W9-AEV-995

DISCARDED

Contemporary French Poetry

Fourteen Witnesses of Man's Fate

Contemporary French Poetry
Fourteen Witnesses of Man's Fate

Edited by Alexander Aspel
and Donald Justice
Introduction by Alexander Aspel
Postface by Paul Engle

Ann Arbor Paperbacks
The University of Michigan Press

First edition as an Ann Arbor Paperback 1965

Library of Congress Catalog Card No. 65-13443
Published in the United States of America by
The University of Michigan Press and simultaneously
in Toronto, Canada, by Ambassador Books Limited
Manufactured in the United States of America

Book design by Quentin Fiore

Permissions

Grateful acknowledgment is made of the permissions granted to reprint the poems in French, as follows:

"Les Traits du ciel," "La Parole descend," "L'Ombre," by Pierre Reverdy, from *Sources du vent*. Editions des Trois Collines, 1946.

"Règle," "L'Allumette," by Francis Ponge, from *Le Grand Recueil*. © Editions Gallimard, 1961.

"L'Huître," by Francis Ponge, from *Le Parti-pris des choses*. © Editions Gallimard, 1942.

"La Souffrance," "La Transcendance irait mal," by Jacques Audiberti, from *Toujours*. © Editions Gallimard, 1943.

"Le Vent," by Henri Michaux, from *La Nuit remue*. © Editions Gallimard, 1935.

"Demain n'est pas encore . . . ," "Après l'accident," by Henri Michaux, from *Face aux verrous*. © Editions Gallimard, 1954.

From "Etendues," and from "Allées et venues," by Jean Follain, from *Tout Instant*. © Editions Gallimard, 1957.

"Tu as bien fait de partir, Arthur Rimbaud," by René Char, from *Fureur et mystère*. © Editions Gallimard, 1948.

"Antonin Artaud," by René Char, from *Les Matinaux*. © Editions Gallimard, 1950.

"Quatre Fascinants," "Victoire éclair," "La Bibliothèque est en feu," "A deux enfants, 1, 2," "L'Eternité à Lourmarin," "Contrevenir," by René Char, from *La Parole en archipel*. © Editions Gallimard, 1962.

"Le Lieu miraculeux de l'amour," "Pays retrouvé," "Qui possède quoi?," by André Frénaud, from *Il n'y a pas de paradis*. © Editions Gallimard, 1962.

From "Elégies" 4 poems, by Guillevic, from *Exécutoire*. © Editions Gallimard, 1947.

"La Couleur du froid," "Le Grand Théâtre," "Haut Lieu," by André Pieyre de Mandiargues, from *Astyanax*. Editions du Terrain Vague, 1957, © Gallimard, 1964.

"Poème d'amour à Hélène," "Celui qui entre par hasard," by René Guy Cadou, from *Hélène ou le règne végétal*. Editions Pierre Seghers, 1952.

"Vrai Nom," by Yves Bonnefoy, from *Du Mouvement et de l'immobilité de Douve*. Mercure de France, 1953.

"Menaces du témoin, I, II, III, IV, V," "A San Francesco, le soir," by Yves Bonnefoy, from *Hier régnant désert*. Mercure de France, 1958.

"Art de la poésie," by Yves Bonnefoy, from *Mercure de France*, June 1963.

From "Le Moteur blanc, VI, X," "En pleine terre," "Le Vin du jour," "Cession," by André du Bouchet, from *Dans la chaleur vacante*. Mercure de France, 1961.

From "Sonnets," "Intérieur," "La Traversée," by Philippe Jaccottet, from *L'Effraie et autres poésies*. © Editions Gallimard, 1953.

"Le Travail du poète," "Le Locataire," by Philippe Jaccottet, from *L'Ignorant*. © Editions Gallimard, 1957.

"Le Règne minéral," "Le Partage," "L'Air," and from "Saccades," by Jacques Dupin, from *Gravir*. © Editions Gallimard, 1963.

A Note on the Translations

By Donald Justice

The poets here translated were chosen by my coeditor, while I am responsible for the choice of translators and translations. All of the translators have been associated with the University of Iowa, as teachers or as students; aside from this they have in common only the fact that most are not professional translators but poets themselves, at various stages of their careers, and as such have —many of them—been members, at one time or another, of the Poetry Workshop.

If an interest in the poetry of other languages may be measured in terms of the number and variety of translations being made, then the American poet has, I think, never shown himself more interested than he is showing himself everywhere today. This collection is, of course, only a small part of the evidence. It is perhaps special in that it has grown out of a program in creative writing of many years' standing; the encouragement such a program can provide in the making of translations, however obvious, is worth emphasizing.

The idea of translation in general embodied here—it is an idea only and by no means intended to achieve the status of a theory—is that meaningful versions of poems in one language can exist in another. These are neither word-for-word prose versions nor "imitations," though each of these kinds of translation can serve a useful purpose. The translations are meant to be readable in English; this does not necessarily signify that they will present no difficulties, for the original texts of some of the poets included are among the most difficult poems written anywhere today, as well as among the most interesting. Most of the translators have tried to preserve the order of the images, the tone, and approximate style of the original, and, where possible, even the special difficulties themselves.

The final texts of certain of these translations would not have been possible without the devoted collaboration of Mme Paulène Aspel and, in some cases, of the poets themselves. Nor would the collection have been possible without the enthusiastic support of the director of the writing program, Paul Engle, whose idea the project originally was. Others who have contributed in several ways during the preparation of the volume and to whom the editors wish to record their sincere gratitude are John C. Weaver, former dean of the Graduate School, Ralph Freedman, head of the Division of Comparative Literature, Edmund Keeley and Mark Strand, first teachers of the Translation Workshop, as well as Mr. Frank Hanlin, Miss Ada Stoflet, Mrs. Lowell Uda, Mrs. Robert Gore, Mrs. Kathy Salyer, Mrs. Marie Wences, Mrs. Caryl Barber, Mrs. Rosalind Sherk, and, most particularly, Miss Dori Katz for their various forms of essential editorial assistance.

Contents

Introduction 1

Pierre Reverdy

Les Traits du ciel (from *Sources du vent*) 20
Features of the Sky 21
La Parole descend (from *Sources du vent*) 22
The Word Comes Down 23
L'Ombre (from *Sources du vent*) 24
The Shadow 25

Francis Ponge

Règle (from *Le Grand Recueil*) 28
Rule 29
L'Allumette (from *Le Grand Recueil*) 30
The Match 31
L'Huître (from *Le Parti-pris des choses*) 32
The Oyster 33

Jacques Audiberti

La Souffrance (from *Toujours*) 34
Suffering 35
La Transcendance irait mal (from *Toujours*) 38
Transcendence Wouldn't Do 39

Henri Michaux

Le Vent (from *La Nuit remue*) 42
The Wind 43

Demain n'est pas encore . . . (from *Face aux verrous*) 44
Tomorrow Is Not Yet . . . 45

Après l'accident (from *Face aux verrous*) 46
After the Accident 47

Jean Follain

from
Etendues (from *Tout Instant*) 52
Extensions 53

from
Allées et venues (from *Tout Instant*) 54
Comings and Goings 55

René Char

Tu as bien fait de partir, Arthur Rimbaud! (from *Fureur et mystère*) 58
You Did Well to Leave, Arthur Rimbaud! 59

Antonin Artaud (from *Les Matinaux*) 60
Antonin Artaud 61

Quatre Fascinants (*from La Parole en archipel*) 62
Four Fascinators 63

Victoire éclair (from *La Parole en archipel*) 66
Lightning Victory 67

La Bibliothèque est en feu (from *La Parole en archipel*) 68
The Library Is on Fire 69

A deux enfants, 1, 2 (from *La Parole en archipel*) 78
For Two Children, 1, 2 79

L'Eternité à Lourmarin (from *La Parole en archipel*) 82
Eternity at Lourmarin 83
Contrevenir (from *La Parole en archipel*) 84
Contravention 85

André Frénaud
Le Lieu miraculeux de l'amour (from *Il n'y a pas de paradis*) 86
The Miraculous Place of Love 87
Pays retrouvé (from *Il n'y a pas de paradis*) 88
Rediscovered Country 89
Qui possède quoi? (from *Il n'y a pas de paradis*) 90
Who Owns What? 91

Guillevic
from
Elégies, 4 poems (from *Exécutoire*) 92
Elegies 93

André Pieyre de Mandiargues
La Couleur du froid (from *Astyanax*) 100
The Color of Cold 101
Le Grand Théâtre (from *Astyanax*) 102
The Big Theater 103
Haut Lieu (from *Astyanax*) 104
High Place 105

René Guy Cadou
Poème d'amour à Hélène (from *Hélène ou le règne végétal*) 106

Love Poem to Helen 107

Celui qui entre par hasard (from *Hélène ou le règne végétal*) 110

Who Risks It Where a Poet Lives 111

Yves Bonnefoy

Vrai Nom (from *Du Mouvement et de l'immobilité de Douve*) 112

True Name 113

Menaces du témoin (from *Hier régnant désert*) 114

Threats of the Witness 115

A San Francesco, le soir (from *Hier régnant désert*) 120

San Francesco, at Night 121

Art de la poésie (from *Mercure de France*) 122

The Art of Poetry 123

André du Bouchet

from

Le Moteur blanc

VI, X (from *Le Moteur blanc*) 124

White Motor, VI, X 125

En pleine terre (from *Le Moteur blanc*) 126

On the Open Earth 127

Le Vin du jour (from *Le Moteur blanc*) 128

The Wine of Day 129

Cession (from *Dans la chaleur vacante*) 130

Surrender 131

Contents

Philippe Jaccottet

from
Quelques Sonnets (from *L'Effraie et autres poésies*) 132
Sonnet 133

Intérieur (from *L'Effraie et autres poésies*) 134
Interior 135

La Traversée (from *L'Effraie et autres poésies*) 136
The Crossing 137

Le Travail du poète (from *L'Ignorant*) 138
The Poet's Work 139

Le Locataire (from *L'Ignorant*) 142
The Tenant 143

Jacques Dupin

Le Règne minéral (from *Gravir*) 144
The Mineral Kingdom 145

Le Partage (from *Gravir*) 146
The Portion 147

L'Air (from *Gravir*) 148
Air 149

from
Saccades (from *Gravir*) 150
Fits and Starts 151

Selective Bibliography 152

Notes on Editors and Translators 185

Postface 190

Introduction

By Alexander Aspel

In the past decade the poetic landscape of France has changed. This change was not caused by any sudden explosion of new schools, such as the short-lived *lettrisme* of the late 1940's, but rather by an uneven process of reshifting produced by the movement of time itself. The creators of the surrealist movement and their contemporaries, born in the last two decades of the nineteenth century, have reached the venerable position of old masters. In their wake, a generation of poets born in the early 1900's has moved up to constitute a middle generation of the leading figures in contemporary poetry. Raymond Queneau (b. 1901), Michel Leiris (b. 1901), and René Char (b. 1907) have acquired a significant following, establishing their historical position. Others of the same age group, less widely noted before, have emerged as major figures of the contemporary scene. Guillevic and André Pieyre de Mandiargues, Jean Follain, and André Frénaud have shaped many essential features of the new poetic situation. At the same time, poets who, near the midcentury, represented the younger generation, Georges Schehadé (b. 1910), Patrice de la Tour du Pin (b. 1911), Jean Grosjean (b. 1912), Edith Boissonnas (b. 1915), Pierre Emmanuel (b. 1916), and others have come to occupy the safer but perhaps less influential position of recognized maturity in joining this middle generation.

The main change, however, occurred when, in a development parallel to the emergence of the new novel, young poets arose in the 1950's and early 1960's, defining the attitudes of the generation born in the 1920's. Among them Yves Bonnefoy and Philippe Jaccottet have established themselves as the recognized leaders of a new intuitive approach to reality, seeking a more immediate and fundamental contact with things within the context of life than they could find in most of the poetry of their direct predecessors. Here belongs to some extent also the posthumous spread of the poetic reputation of René Guy Cadou (1920–1951). André du Bouchet and Jacques Dupin, each in a personal way, have lent significant support to the same trend—the work of Char and of Pierre Reverdy appearing to have been the mainspring of this line of poetry. Still younger talents have distinguished themselves recently without, however, modifying significantly as yet the present poetic situation.

Intended to reflect the changing perspective of the 1960's, the selection of poets translated in this volume focuses on the major poets of the middle and younger generations. But it also includes poets of the older age group whose influence appears today proportionately more active than it was some time ago. These are Pierre Reverdy, Francis Ponge, Jacques Audiberti, and Henri Michaux, with whom the selection begins. Léon-Paul Fargue and Pierre-Jean Jouve are often associated with the new poetry of today, but could be excluded from this selection because they are already well represented in earlier anthologies.* Saint-John Perse, whose poetry gained new actuality and an even wider audience in 1961, with the award of the Nobel Prize, is similarly well known in America through anthologies and full-length translations of his work.

Besides the above considerations, the selection of authors and of their poems was determined by the literary merit of the translations. Many poets of the middle generation mentioned above had to be excluded because, within the time limits for the completion of the book, translations did not become available from the translators chosen. The same reason applies concerning the particular poems translated from each author. The content of the volume reflects a compromise between a wider initial selection and the quality and quantity of translations achieved. These circumstances, it is hoped, permit this anthology to reflect the response of a whole group of young American poets to the promise and challenge of one of the most vigorous creative centers of the world today.

Like their surrealist predecessors and contemporaries, the poets of this selection are mostly the direct descendants of the Rimbaud of the radical quest of the true life

*Cf. *Mid-Century French Poets*, edited by Wallace Fowlie (New York: Grove Press, 1954); *The Penguin Book of French Verse, The Twentieth Century*, edited by Anthony Hartley (Penguin, 1959); *French Poetry from Baudelaire to the Present*, edited by Elaine Marks (New York: Laurel Language Library, 1962).

and of that other self who is absent. Unlike surrealists, but as direct descendants of Baudelaire, they have an acute sense of human fragility and limitation, of the obstacles separating this quest from its goal. This awareness leads their poetry to new tensions, but also to new forms of poetic vision and expression. A fundamental uncertainty about man and his world is wed in many of them to a need of fulfillment which is less than a hope and more than a conviction. It no longer takes their poetry into the realm of pure poetry, as it did with Mallarmé, Valéry, and their immediate successors, but into a direct relationship with things, matter, inner demons, or everyday events. Yet unlike the "engaged poetry" of the World War II and postwar period, theirs remains apart from contemporary social and political concerns. It seeks fresh contact with reality beyond the concepts of established awareness and creeds, aiming at new evidences of permanent values, of Being, of a presence felt as sacred. Immediacy of experience and of expression is their main concern, but it is an immediacy controlled by lucid and inquisitive minds.

The traditional forms of poetry reasserted by Paul Valéry, as well as those ample forms of poetic celebration and praise, consecrated earlier by Paul Claudel, Saint-John Perse, and many poets of the immediate postwar period, are shunned by the poets of this movement, except when these forms serve some rebellious intention, as in Audiberti's poetry, or coincide with exceptionally serene themes, as occasionally in the poetry of Philippe Jaccottet. The typical forms of this poetry are free verse and prose poems or regular verse devoid of rhyme or supported only by oblique rhymes and faint echoes of sound. This poetry avoids apparent symmetries of form, but for that reason all the more intensely seeks broken and mobile patterns of stylization. Yet instead of loosening the structure of the poem these devices tend to strengthen it, doubtless because they are based on a concentration of poetic power on images that aim beyond the conceptual limits of language so as to convey some unnamed intuition. The surrealist conquest of the free image has been fully exploited by these poets, who have made the image the nucleus of a new art of concentric penetration into the unknown.

Poets of the Selection

Among the poets of the surrealist generation, the attitude toward life and poetry of PIERRE REVERDY (1889–1960) represents and foretells perhaps most pertinently the direction the new poetry was to take after World War II, especially in the 1950's and 1960's. Surrealist poetic revolt was intended to change life; the function of poetry for Reverdy was, on the contrary, to live the given life at its utmost point of authenticity, at the sharp edge between dream and reality, trying to catch the fleeting instants where reality could meet the absolute. Reverdy assumed entirely in his poetry the misery of man's fate, he laid it bare in hard and short sentences and direct images that have an ominous ring because they are separated from any comforting human context and devoid of any reference to personal existence. An anonymous, searching, and uneasy soul looks at the world through these fragmentary visions, as if they had a secret to reveal. But the secret is never caught, the poet's vision is constantly blocked by an invisible screen. Yet, induced by certain faint sensations—a breath of wind, the crunch of snow, a reflection in the window—he starts over and over again, fixing these fleeting instants of promise and refusal as immediate sense perceptions in poems of unusual density. Reverdy has called such poetry of direct perception *poésie brute* ("raw poetry").

Francis Ponge (1899–) has adopted the method of a meticulous and objective observer of things in the outside world, which he describes not by the elliptic technique of a visionary witness, as did Reverdy, but in the exact terms of a rational yet lyrical observer. Each thing described is seen as a world in itself, divorced from the human world. We recognize in these things the working of our own fundamental needs, desires, and fears, but a cool distance reduces the current of empathy to the sheer awareness that such phenomena are present. Reverdy's bare perceptions carried a current of impersonal communication, they implied some faint transcendence; Ponge's objective lyricism stops and encloses the things in their own particular essence, admirable in itself. When penetrated by the prying and playful mind of the observer, as the oyster is forced open, it reveals only more delicate, more admirable layers of the same autonomous essence. The cool admiration produced by the poem may stand, however, for a significant link of the aesthetic *modus vivendi* with the universe. As in Reverdy's poetry, it is a universe of fragments, "the feathers of Mallarmé's icy swan scattered in space," as the poet Jaccottet has described them. The art that conveys this world of isolated yet radiant things has a tone of lucid discretion and the dry grace of perfect drawings.

With Jacques Audiberti (1899–), on the contrary, the full-bodied word, carried aloft by rich rhymes, comes to new life in a poetry of savage and despairing exaltation, uniting Victor Hugo's verbal exuberance with the surrealist aesthetic of the incongruous. But in Audiberti such a yielding of the creative initiative to words is a conscious strategy of the poet and leads occasionally to poems of supreme density, vibrating with tensions of love, hate, and menaced pride not unrelated to Mallarmé's aesthetics. The whole realm of polyvalent images liberated by modern poetry seems to be captured in these poems, conveying a sensation of nearly unbearable fullness which is equivalent in the poet's intention to the neutralizing power of silence.

Henri Michaux (1899–) shares with Audiberti the surrealist appeal to violent imagery, his sense for the magic force of words, as well as his poetic shrewdness, which aims at the neutralization of inner tensions by the very energy of imaginary outbursts. (Michaux calls this function of his poetry *exorcisme.*) Yet in Michaux's poetry—verse and poetic prose alike—these outbursts are under the strict control of a profoundly rebellious, skeptical, and ironic mind, which sharpens and stylizes them into distinctly perceived clusters of turbulence. These are held at a distance—often in the guise of weird allegorical figures that remain nightmarish and demoniac—occasionally forcing the very language of the poem beyond the reasonable limits of the French tongue. At other times these outbursts soften into limpid reflections on the common phenomena of nature and life, where only an infrequent swell of rhythm and a few disturbing images betray the underlying pressures of refusal and horror in the face of existence.

JEAN FOLLAIN (1903–), whose consistent production has brought him gradually to the front line of contemporary poetry, has little in common with the surrealist tradition. He appears to have taken his main directions from Léon-Paul Fargue's and Max Jacob's art of the fabulous as disclosed in commonplace things and events, blending the refinement of the former with the cordial simplicity of the latter. The world described in Follain's poems—verse or prose—is mainly a world of childhood memories from a rural small town, twice remote from the metropolitan present of the poet, slowed down by distance and fixed in a ceremonial order transgressing time and personal existence. The minute precision of Follain's descriptions might relate his things-past to Ponge's objects, were they not steeped in the uncertain light of a dream suggesting mysterious extensions beyond themselves, being, as the poet says, "open to the event." Modest in their presence, they open inadvertently on some transcendence, which may be conveyed by a mere change of light or a unique cry of contentment, heard once, existing forever. The tragic tension of promise and refusal, characteristic of Reverdy's poetry of faint transcendence, yields, in Follain's poems, to a mood of discreet expectation before the unknown in things, foreshadowing Guillevic's impersonal communion with matter.

RENÉ CHAR (1907–), the youngest among the prominent poets that participated actively in the surrealist movement (1929–37), has inherited from his surrealist experience an unusual sense for the compelling power of free and open images, free from reasonable connotations, open to possible future or forgotten magical resources in the words, which he puts to work in a new form of elliptic poem (in verse or prose) leading often to short aphoristic statements. Char inaugurates a postsurrealist phase of intensified poetic communion with life and nature. Fundamental humanistic values (love, beauty, justice, fraternity, personal integrity, a sense of elevation and nobility) are reasserted here, in a mood of exasperated serenity. Like his friend Albert Camus, René Char recreates the ethics of modern man, but he grounds them on a deeper level of poetic mystery, where he experiences them as a sudden revelation of essences, as a manifestation of the sacred, as a strength of existence. Any event, the most common occurrence, can be a hint, a promise of such an illumination, if not a revelation itself. Such are Char's "Fascinators." Fragments as they are, these "lightning instants," which frequently unite vehement contradictions, constitute rigorous wholes. Built around a compelling image, a long poem like "The Library Is on Fire" unites them closely into an *ars poetica,* which is at the same time a total vision of the world. Yet instead of being connected by logical or emotional links, these fragments are held together by the very energy of their juxtaposition. Similarly, Char's images draw much of their power from the sudden meeting of words stripped of all traditional support.

Char's figure, backed by his fame as a resistance fighter, presently towers above his generation as a historical landmark denoting if not a reconciliation of the surrealist revolt with the condition of existence, at least a poetic bridge between the contradictions in man, between him and the world. A new sensual trust and a new feeling of concrete space are suggested. Things, human figures, and landscapes emerge. Baudelaire's series of beacons is extended—to Rimbaud, to Artaud—all proofs of a difficult but possible dignity of life, based on man's creative freedom. Some links are thus established with the poetry of Reverdy on the one hand, and Ponge on the other, but above all with the younger poets who take directions connected with them.

The poetry of André Frénaud (1907–   ), a latecomer on the literary scene who has reached prominence in the 1950's and 1960's, is derived also from the quest for communion with the world and with its Being, confusedly foreseen, yet elusive and treacherous. Despairing to reach it, yet resolved to clarify its approaches in terms of earthly evidence, Frénaud ends up by testifying in its favor, by the very failure of his quest, or rather by the obstinate repetition of his failures. As a Sisyphus of man's misery, he brings forward negative evidence of man's dignity, shown to be in the final analysis a "purposeless passion," to echo J.-P. Sartre's famous definition. Frénaud also shares with the existentialist approach his poetic method of repeated poking and digging, the use of all possible forms—from long descriptive poems to short aphorisms and prose pieces—avoiding purposely too evidently harmonious patterns, rhymes, and alexandrine verse.

Guillevic (1907–), poet of elementary matter, has abolished personal humanity even from his own name, depriving himself of a first name in choosing to be known by his surname only. Yet this impersonal poet, an adept of materialism and intellectually akin to Ponge, does not lose himself in matter, but continues its conquest by naming what has no name. Remote from Ponge's objective rationalism, closer to Follain's opening outward to things, Guillevic's approach is rather through a quasi-mystic communion, through a loving and suffering empathy, with matter. He is most powerfully attracted by its earthiest forms, by the hard, dark core of rocks, the sluggish depths of caves, sensing in them the original home of man, and for that matter of the foundation of his poetic imagination. The primitivistic tendencies of modern art become here an imaginary penetration of the elements through the magic power of words. As in many contemporaries, these powers are condensed and ordered in precise images, devoid of loose emotionalism, often bordering on epigrammatic concision.

ANDRÉ PIEYRE DE MANDIARGUES (1909–), also a latecomer in his generation, who joined André Breton and the remaining surrealist group only after World War II, shares with his generation the attitude of an apparently impersonal witness of the world. The world unfolded by his verse and prose poems is also, like that of Ponge and Guillevic, a world of external things, but of singular things, stemming from a surrealist vision, arranged in a fabulous setting and watched by a fascinated eye. Yet, unlike the artificially theatrical world of Jean Cocteau's poetry, Mandiargues' has a secretive and dreamy quality in spite or indeed perhaps because of a great precision in rendering the detail of objects. Such neatness of design and color, combined with the ritualistic nature of acts committed in this magic setting, invests things and figures with an ominous glow, suggestive of some sacred significance. Hatred and love, death and life, eroticism and purity, black and red, find in Mandiargues' poems their subtle and stirring agreements.

The new poetry of today, of poets born in the twenties, begins with the elegiac lyrics of RENÉ GUY CADOU (1920–51) whose early death interrupted his production but not the spread of his work. After so many years of poetic revolt and despair, René Cadou's confident poetry was felt as a refreshing return to "natural" sources of poetry, to a gently loving heart, to a warm relationship with oneself and the world. It was also a return to simplicity and modesty in expression, but to a simplicity that had absorbed Guillaume Apollinaire's art of capturing the shiver of fleeting sensations and to some extent also Reverdy's aesthetics of the bare image, of what he called *poésie brute*.

Cadou's poetry does not represent, however, the dominating trend of the new generation, whose main spokesman at present, according to all evidence, is YVES BONNEFOY (1923–), author of a new kind of austere and searching poetry, intended to stretch the powers of French poetic language not only beyond its conceptual limits but perhaps beyond the evocative function of the image itself. Poetry to Bonnefoy is above all a renewal of the existing poetic idiom, a creation of a new language, not by purification, as Mallarmé intended it, but by an integration of intuitive evidences of reality. René Char had carried the expressive resources of the image, definitely freed by the surrealists, to their most intense power of poetic synthesis, bridging the contradictions of experience through flashing unification of the contraries. Bonnefoy does not content himself, however, with the "lightning victories" of perfect moments. He looks for a more permanent basis for his poetry and seems to have found it in an intuition of life and reality, not felt any longer as opposed to or separated from, but as integrating, death and oblivion. Thus, he reaches directly back to "the new light that death sheds on life" evidenced by Baudelaire's *Flowers of Evil,* according to Bonnefoy's own words. To Bonnefoy, however, this new light is the very light of "sacred presence," the only sacred light possible for men who have lost the sense of divine presence. The rift that the preceding generations have tried to bridge or to cross by the magic of poetic words does not appear to Bonnefoy any more as a temporary crisis of conscience which could be cured by better times or a more efficient language, but as the very essence of reality, as the sign of temporal existence that authenticates it. And yet this sign, this presence cannot be named. It escapes any conceptual definition, it can only be intuitively surrounded, not caught, only attracted and hinted at by the imagination in instants of suffering, nostalgia, or uneasiness. The resulting poetry has a muffled and yet solemn sound. It avoids formal perfection, as a trap of artificiality; it elaborates carefully its own unfinished harmonies and in words releases powers not simply of ambiguous or contradictory aggression, nor of crystal-like purity, but of a diffuse and somber light that permeates reality, matter, and soul. It suggests the dark light of the void, but of a potent void that is permanently active and able to sustain man's life. Such in Bonnefoy's poetry is the light of "the lifeless face," of a memory that continues through oblivion, or of "the stone that hides the secret church." Thus, the very testimony of the poetic witness is a menace. The aesthetics of this poetry has been formulated by the poet himself in the sentence: "Imperfection is the Peak."

André du Bouchet (1924–) has carried the distrust of established forms and concepts of existence to the utmost limits of refusal, rejecting as offering no valid ground for poetic truth those externals of experience which concern the poet's social and practical self, the upper layers of his personality, and certain forms of his own critical consciousness. "I am writing as far away as possible from myself," "I must struggle against my own noise," the poet says, joining the line of impersonal, yet subjective poets. This radical position has led to a poetry of abrupt and elliptic statements closely related to René Char's aesthetic of aphoristic condensation and tension, and sharing with Reverdy and Bonnefoy an acute awareness of the obstacles placed in the way of ultimate foundations or direct communion with things. In his quest for immediacy, Du Bouchet, even more radically than Reverdy, has reduced the elements of his poetry to moments of utter bareness. A few galvanic images (fire, air, wind, rock, a wall, a tree, the red, the white), no longer felt as definable shapes or as mere hints of the beyond, but as primitive forces at work, suddenly release an intense sensation of coming to grips with a decisive event. This may be a moment of close communion with the absolute through fire or a white light, but it is a harsh communion, abolishing all particular forms of existence. More often, the communion is refused or choked off, but the very negation speaks strongly in favor of the fire or the wind of transcendence. Thus, the wall, in "Surrender," takes over the function of the wind. Images and themes become reversible, disclosing a harrowing contradiction in the fact of existence. There is no solution for the poet. He is condemned to be torn and yet to continue his austere quest, through words grounded on and surrounded by huge blocks of silence, suggested on Du Bouchet's pages by the very arrangement of lines on paper.

The discreet and elegiac poetry of PHILIPPE JACCOTTET (1925–) links the poetics of his generation with a humanistic tradition less shaken by the surrealistic commotion than that of the immediately preceding poets. It indeed borders more often on Rilke, Eliot, Valéry, perhaps Supervielle, than on Eluard, Artaud, or Breton; yet it shares with René Char's the call of dawns carrying a promise of fresh beginnings and the passion of poetic ethics for man. A feeling of frailty, shadow, and void in a secretly threatened reality underlies Jaccottet's reaction to the world. His diction has a limpid quality, an ease in motion and a light grace producing effects of transparency and discreet serenity. Like the other poets of this selection, Jaccottet is not a poet of self-confession or mere self-assertion, but a witness of the world and of man's condition. The space he moves in is also a world of everyday occurrences, of common things—perceived, however, not at moments of violent immediacy or cool distance, but rather of human closeness, of reflexive intimacy. A rare gift of unpossessive love, of self-effacing attention to the world suffuses his poetry of frail reflections with vibrating life. The moving shapes of the world's beauty pierce the shadow, to hint at Beauty itself.

Sometimes, before the shadow closes in again, the poet listens to the faint breath of God in an open sky. Death itself softens, changes into the "damp house of plants."

JACQUES DUPIN (1927–) has reached in his latest collections of poems a strength and a unity of expression which make his work one of the significant recent contributions to French poetry. Partaking of the feeling of an inwardly shattered world, Dupin joins the aesthetics and the poetic quest of Du Bouchet, Bonnefoy, and René Char. His world also is a world of crisis, of harsh contradictions and aggressive challenge. Out of the crumbling confusion inherent in reality, the poem seeks to extricate something that survives it, an affirmation, a promise, a presence, the sheer desire of a "frugal road," or the need to assert and shelter the poet's own integrity. Says Dupin: "I write in order to bury my gold." But in his imaginary world, burial is also seeding, similar to lightning which makes "stone spring up and grow," death being birth. Dupin also experiences negation and contradiction as basic qualities of reality, but it seems that in his poetry the opposites united are unable or unwilling to blend or to fuse, nor do they destroy each other. On the contrary, they are mutually activated, maintaining the poem in a state of unresolved trembling. Abrupt slopes, spikes, splinters, fractures, and crevasses, all forms of hostile rupture, so frequent in Dupin's poetry, contribute to this tension, which, as J.-P. Richard suggests, had established already in Rimbaud's poetry the basis of a deeper consonance, preparing the way for contact with the totality of life, with the sacred. The usual themes of poetic endeavor (woman, love, night, sea) are experienced in this context as elemental forces ("the back of your neck, more base than stone," "anfractuous loves") whose turmoil, laying us bare, gives access to "the dew to come."

"What you left in silence, I hear," Jacques Dupin says in a poem to Reverdy, after the latter's death. Du Bouchet speaks, in the same context, of "that *nothing* which cannot disappear . . . that which takes shape when everything we can imagine has come to an end, that is, indeed, the inexhaustible reality, which Reverdy has spotted as has no one else. And he has laid bare its advent."

Thus, the youngest poets join hands with the oldest one, already gone, defining at the same time many essential features of the new art of poetry as illustrated in this book. It is a poetry neither of despair nor of fulfillment, but of search, approach, and expectation. At its peak, it is a poetry of advent. Here poetry is not an end in itself, but a means of apprehending a reality more fundamental than the disintegrating profusion of appearances. Moving beyond surrealism, it anticipates the concept of a realism in depth.

The poet, stripped of his accidental self, withdraws to the position of an impersonal, yet subjective—passionate, fascinated, or simply waking—witness of man's fate, of his relation with a world laid equally bare. Submitting to what he can sense, he discovers rather than invents.

The poem, a fragment of the poet's experience, unites contradictory and elusive instants of intuition. New, essentially dynamic forms of poetic synthesis are thus produced, ranging from "secret churches" to "lightning victories." Yet the concise unity of these poems is not a closed one. In all of them, silence, which is so potently explored in Reverdy, Char, Bonnefoy, Du Bouchet, and, with paradoxical loudness, in Audiberti, acts as a necessary corollary of images and opens the poem to "the event," to that "nothing which cannot disappear," and "lies ahead of the poem." Even Ponge's autonomous objects refer, in their own discreet way, through their inner radiation and play of suggestions, to what is next, and perhaps beyond. By dint of things present, the poet discovers the possible.

Les Traits du ciel

Le feu qui danse
L'oiseau qui chante
Le vent qui meurt
Les vagues de la glace
Et les flots de rumeur

Dans l'oreille les cris lointains
du jour qui passe
toutes les flammes lasses
la voix du voyageur

Toute la poudre au ciel
Le talon sur la terre
L'œil fixé sur la route
Où les pas sont inscrits
Que le nombre déroule
Aux noms qui sont partis

Dans les plis des nuages
le visage inconnu
Celui que l'on regarde
Et qui n'est pas venu

Pierre Reverdy

Features of the Sky

Fire that dances
Bird that sings
Wind that dies
        The waves of ice
        And the tides of rumor

Faraway cries in the ear
            from the dying day
    all those tired flames
    the voice of the traveler

All the dust in the sky
    The heel on the ground
The eye glued to the road
    Where footsteps are engraved
Whose number unrolls
    To names that have left

In the creases of the clouds
            the unknown face
The one we look at
    And who didn't come

Pierre Reverdy
Translated by
Joseph de Roche

La Parole descend

Tous les coquelicots ou les lèvres des femmes
reflétés dans le ciel

Il a plu
Les enfants se noient sur le trottoir
Et le flot de la rue
La ville en entonnoir

De profil la journée glisse vers le couchant
Le pavé se descelle
Et les bêtes craintives
au bruit que fait le vent
s'en vont
Et elles s'appellent

Sur les balcons les vitres tremblent
—un moment—
La maison a la fièvre
5 heures
à part la nuit qui se mêle au tournant

Les arbres en prières

Pierre Reverdy

The Word Comes Down

All poppies or lips of women
reflected in the sky

It's been raining
Children drown on the sidewalk
And the floods of the street
The city a funnel

The day glides sideways toward sleep
A paving stone unfastens itself
And the timid beasts
at the noise of the wind
run away
And call out

Window panes flash on the balcony
—an instant—
The house runs a fever
5 o'clock
save for night which is joining the street corner

The trees at worship

Pierre Reverdy
Translated by Joseph de Roche

L'Ombre

Un homme
Et je suis celui-là

Sur le mur
Un profil s'abat
Silhouette décapitée

La porte tranche le mot
le corps
Ta figure décomposée
Triste nouvelle
Une larme dans ta prunelle
Un peu d'eau
Ah! que ton front caché sous ton chapeau
est comme ton cœur

Une lueur
Une perle au bout des doigts

Un mot doucement reste comme un oiseau
Sur les lèvres
Perché
Perdu

The Shadow

A man
And I'm that man

On the wall
A shadow tumbles down
Silhouette, the head lopped off

The door slams on the word
the body
Your distorted face
Unhappy message
A tear deep in the eye
A drop
Ah! hidden under your hat your face
is like your heart

A flashing
A pearl at the fingertips

Gently a word stays like a bird
On the lips
Perched
Lost

Un fruit reste pendu
En passant ta main l'a arraché

Des gouttes de sang chaud
Coulent doucement dans la nuit
Un homme celui-là n'a pas encore dormi

Pierre Reverdy

A fruit still hangs
Your hand in passing tore it away

Drops of warm blood
Flow softly off in the night
A man, that man, has yet to sleep

Pierre Reverdy
Translated by Joseph de Roche

Règle

C'est trop de la neige
à cause que chère
aux cartes postales.

Préférez le gel,
le gel et le vent
sans nuage au ciel,

le sérum, l'acide
et le frais d'avis
pour vos yeux vitreux,

pour vos doigts fragiles,
et pour le discret
escargot du sexe.

Francis Ponge

Rule

One's had enough of
the snow so dear
to postal cards.

Better the frost,
the frost and the wind
with no cloud in the sky,

the serum, the acid,
and fresh air in the face
for your glassy eyes,

for your delicate fingers,
and for the discreet
snail of sex.

Francis Ponge
Translated by
Donald Justice

L'Allumette

Le feu faisait un corps à l'allumette.
Un corps vivant, avec ses gestes,
son exaltation, sa courte histoire.
Les gaz émanés d'elle flambaient,
lui donnaient ailes et robes, un corps même:
une forme mouvante,
émouvante.

Ce fut rapide.

La tête seulement a pouvoir de s'enflammer, au contact d'une réalité dure,
—et l'on entend alors comme le pistolet du starter.
Mais, dès qu'elle a pris,
la flamme
—en droite ligne, vite et la voile penchée comme un bateau de régate—
parcourt tout le petit bout de bois,

Qu'à peine a-t-elle viré de bord
finalement elle laisse
aussi noir qu'un curé.

Francis Ponge

The Match

Fire gave the match a body.
A body alive, with its gestures,
its exaltation, its brief story.
The emanating gases flamed up,
gave it wings and gowns, even a body:
a shape in motion,
and moving.

It was quick.

Only the head can burst into flames, in contact with
a harsh reality,
—and it's heard then like a starter's pistol.
But the moment it's caught,
the flame,
—in a straight line, swiftly, and the sail dipping
like a schooner's—
runs up the sliver of wood,

Which, as soon as it has tacked
it leaves at last
black as a priest.

Francis Ponge
Translated by Clark Blaise

L'Huître

L'huître, de la grosseur d'un galet moyen, est d'une apparence plus rugueuse, d'une couleur moins unie, brillamment blanchâtre. C'est un monde opiniâtrement clos. Pourtant on peut l'ouvrir: il faut alors la tenir au creux d'un torchon, se servir d'un couteau ébréché et peu franc, s'y reprendre à plusieurs fois. Les doigts curieux s'y coupent, s'y cassent les ongles: c'est un travail grossier. Les coups qu'on lui porte marquent son enveloppe de ronds blancs, d'une sorte de halos.

A l'intérieur l'on trouve tout un monde, à boire et à manger: sous un *firmament* (à proprement parler) de nacre, les cieux d'en-dessus s'affaissent sur les cieux d'en-dessous, pour ne former qu'une mare, un sachet visqueux et verdâtre, qui flue et reflue à l'odeur et à la vue, frangé d'une dentelle noirâtre sur les bords.

Parfois très rare une formule perle à leur gosier de nacre, d'où l'on trouve aussitôt à s'orner.

Francis Ponge

The Oyster

The size of a handy pebble, the oyster is coarser looking and, though of a less clear-cut coloring, brilliantly chalkish. It is a stubborn, closed world. Still, it can be opened: you have to put it in the fold of a rag, start in on it with a rugged and slightly crooked blade, keep at it for several tries. The prying fingers get sliced, the fingernails are snapped off: it is a rough kind of work. The pounding you have to give it stamps its casing with white rings, a sort of halo.

Once there on the inside you find a whole world, food and drink: under a *firmament* (literally speaking) of mother-of-pearl the sky above sags over the sky below, forming no more than a small pond, a viscous greenish bag, that rises and ebbs in sights, in smells, fringed with a blackish lace along the edges.

On rare occasions, within the nacreous throat, a little form becomes a pearl, with which to adorn yourself at once.

Francis Ponge
Translated by Tod Perry

La Souffrance

La danseuse danse. La danse
ne danse pas.
La danse est immobile au centre de la danse.
La guerre est immobile au milieu des combats.

Le silence parle. Silence!
"Je ne suis pas
quand surgit un silence outre moi le silence,
chars et canons à bloc zéro dans leur fracas."

On souffre. Souffrir, la souffrance
n'y songe pas.
Elle réclame tout, sauf soi sur sa potence.
Absente de l'étoile où tu la dénommas,

que la souffrance, vieille lance,
gerbe de croix,
voie . . . un figuier, grandeur, bourgeonne, intelligence . . .
qu'elle voie et la griffe, et la goutte, et le gras,

qu'elle voie . . . or d'où, la puissance
lui vient, de voir? . . .
qu'elle voie homme et Dieu rongés par leur essence
et devant l'os vivant les rats, gourmands, s'asseoir,

Suffering

The dancer dances. The dance
does not dance.
The dance is motionless at the center of the dance.
War is motionless at the heart of battle.

The silence speaks. Silence!
"I do not exist
when a silence rises beyond the silence which is me,
tanks and cannons at full blast, but zero in their noise."

People suffer. As for suffering, suffering
does not consider it.
She demands everything, except herself on the gallows.
Absent from the star where you named her,

when suffering, an old spear,
a sheaf of crosses,
sees . . . a fig tree, grandeur, buds, intelligence . . .
when she sees the claw, and the drop, and the fat,

when she sees . . . but where did she get it,
this power to see? . . .
when she sees man and God gnawed away by their
essence
and in front of the live bone the rats, gluttonous, sitting
down,

alors, subite, la souffrance
tremble de soi.
Elle entreprend sa téméraire connaissance.
Ses ongles dans sa chair défigurent la loi.

Tu rencontreras la souffrance.
Tu l'aimeras.
Tu l'aimeras toute arrachée à l'innocence.
Elle pleure. Elle a soif. Elle mange ses bras.

A mesure qu'elle s'avance
vers le plus bas
le monde délivré danse, et la danse danse.
La guerre brait de peur devant l'eau des combats.

Jacques Audiberti

then, of a sudden, suffering
trembles within herself.
She undertakes her daring voyage of self-discovery.
Her nails in her flesh disfigure the law.

You will meet suffering.
You will love her.
You will love her wrested completely from innocence.
She weeps. She is thirsty. She eats her arms.

As she advances
towards the lowest place
the saved world dances, and the dance dances.
War brays from fear in front of the water of battle.

Jacques Audiberti
Translated by Mark Strand

La Transcendance irait mal

Mon père, vous m'avez donné ce qui vous manque,
l'espace où ressentir la fin de la puissance.
Si tu nais, si tu meurs sous le masque de moi,
ainsi faut-il, père du monstre et de l'immonde,
qu'au plus bas de ton souffle, au bout noir de ta sonde,
je m'enfle, je m'exalte et je m'ausculte toi.

Pareil, quand le serpent, que l'arbre chaud démontre,
me presse d'usurper ta face, il te rencontre.
A te déposséder lui me tente avec toi.
Tu tiens que mon amour comble notre distance.
Satan de mon orgueil enrichit ta substance.
Votre bible une et double écrit toute ma loi.

Seigneur du ciel et de l'enfer, que j'entrelace,
ta seule épouse, où dort le soleil de la glace,
où le bleu révélé, le rouge que j'accroîs
forment dans le silence, au plus fort des musiques,
l'ineffable charbon des absences physiques
et le centre absolu du cercle de la croix,

ta seule épouse, à quoi ton myrte infranchissable
accorde une douceur qui fuit vers notre sable
et sous les lacs de l'œil recommence parfois,
celle qui te survit lorsque tu te rétractes
derrière ton secret, l'ennemi de tes actes,
celle qui te nourrit depuis que tu me vois,

Transcendence Wouldn't Do

My father, what thou lackst thou givest me,
space to endure the end of potency.
Since it's my mask your birth and death come through,
then surely, father of deformed and foul,
under your breath and probe's dark tip, I swell,
exalt, and auscultate myself in you.

So, when the snake the warm tree demonstrates
prompts me to take your face, it's you he meets.
He uses you to tempt me to your loss.
You hold that my love overflows our farness.
The devil has enriched you with my pride.
Thy Bible, one and twofold, writes my laws.

Lord of heaven and hell, whom I enlace,
your single bride, where sunlight sleeps in ice,
where red increased by me, blue you reveal
form in silence louder than any music
the sayless ember of the body's absence
and the dead center of the cross's wheel;

your single bride, whom your wild myrtles send
a sweetness to that runs towards our sand
and, in the eyes' lakes, may be renewed;
she who survives you when you go away
behind your secret, hostile to your acts;
she who, when you regard me, brings you food;

ta seule épouse, ô Dieu que ton diable environne,
c'est ta gloire! C'est la sueur de ta couronne!
Elle advient à combler ton miracle désert.
Au delà de mon heure et de mon aptitude
elle plane et se plaît devant ta solitude.
Ensemble, nous l'aimons, mais, toi, comme la chair,

la chair de femme. Ici lorsque je l'articule
au-dessus du fracas du monde minuscule,
moi qui n'offre de toi que le bord menacé,
le fil entre ton verbe et la forme du crime,
je la crée.
Oui, je crée, à la dent de la rime,
l'ivresse de l'odeur de ton flanc tracassé.

Jacques Audiberti

your single bride, O God your Satan binding,
she is your crown's sweat! your grace abounding!
She soars in joy before your solitude
beyond my hour and ability.
She comes to throng your lonely miracle.
We love her, both, but you, as flesh and blood,

as woman's flesh. And when I say it here
above the uproar of this minion sphere
(a menaced verge is all I can provide,
a hair between your verb and active crime),
I cause her.
Yes, I cause, by tooth of rhyme,
the heady odor of your wounded side.

Jacques Audiberti
Translated by Harry Duncan

Le Vent

Le vent essaie d'écarter les vagues de la mer. Mais les vagues tiennent à la mer, n'est-ce pas évident, et le vent tient à souffler . . . non, il ne tient pas à souffler, même devenu tempête ou bourrasque il n'y tient pas. Il tend aveuglément, en fou, et en maniaque vers un endroit de parfait calme, de bonace, où il sera enfin tranquille, tranquille.

Comme les vagues de la mer lui sont indifférentes! Qu'elles soient sur la mer ou sur un clocher, ou dans une roue dentée ou sur la lame d'un couteau, peu lui chaut. Il va vers un endroit de quiétude et de paix où il cesse enfin d'être vent.

Mais son cauchemar dure déjà depuis longtemps.

Henri Michaux

The Wind

The wind tries to part the waves from the sea. But isn't it evident that the waves are bent on the sea and the wind is bent on blowing . . . no, he is not bent on blowing, even having become storm and squall, he is not bent on it. He strives blindly, as a madman and as a maniac for a place of perfect calm, of lull, where he can finally be still, still.

How indifferent he is to the waves of the sea. Whether they are on the sea or on a steeple, or in a cogwheel or on a knife-blade, little he cares. He moves toward a place of quietude and peace where he can finally stop being wind.

But his nightmare has already lasted a long time.

Henri Michaux
Translated by Dori Katz

Demain n'est pas encore . . .

Roule, roule, sort à deux têtes,
roule, houle profonde,
sortie des planètes de nos corps emmaillés.

Soleil pour les retards,
sommeil d'ébène,
sein de mon fruit d'or.

Etendus,
nous embrassons l'orage,
nous embrassons l'espace,

nous embrassons le flot, le ciel, les mondes,
tout avec nous aujourd'hui tenons embrassé,
faisant l'amour sur l'échafaud.

Henri Michaux

Tomorrow Is Not Yet . . .

Turn, turn, two-headed fortune,
turn, deep surge,
sprung from the planets of our swaddled bodies.

Sun for delay,
ebony sleep,
bosom of my gold fruit.

Stretched out,
we embrace the storm,
we embrace space,

we embrace the flood, the sky, the worlds,
everything with us today hold in our embrace
making love on the scaffold.

Henri Michaux
Translated by Dori Katz and
Donald Justice

Après l'accident

Le problème de la nuit reste entier. Comment la traverser, chaque fois la traverser tout entière?

Que mes secondes sont lourdes! Jamais je ne les aurais crues si lourdes. Instants éléphantiasiques.

Loin de tout, rien en vue et pourtant comme des bruits à travers un filtre . . .

J'entends des paroles ininterrompues, comme si sans cesse on disait, on répétait: Labrador, Labrador, Labrador, Labrador, Labrador, Labrador.

Une poche me brasse. Pas de fond. Pas de portes, et moi comme un long boa égaré. J'ai perdu même mes ennemis.

Oh espace, espace abstrait.

Calme, calme qui roule des trains. Calme monumentalement vide. Plus de pointe. Quille poussée. Quille bercée.

Evanoui à la terre . . .

. . . .

Courant froid sous moi, courant chaud dessus.

Fatigué de monter, vais-je descendre? Mais je ne suis plus fatigué. Je ne sais plus rien de ce qui est la fatigue. Je ne la connais plus.

Je suis grand. Je suis tout ce qu'il y a de plus grand. Le seul peut-être tout à fait grand.

Où sont les êtres?

After the Accident

The problem of the night remains total. How to cross it, cross it completely each time?

How heavy my seconds are! I never would have thought them so heavy. Elephantasiac moments.

Far from everything, nothing in sight and yet like noises through a filter . . .

I hear uninterrupted words, as though someone were endlessly saying, repeating: Labrador, Labrador, Labrador, Labrador, Labrador, Labrador.

A pocket stirs me up. No bottom. No doors, and I, like a long boa, wandering. I've lost even my enemies.

Oh space, abstract space.

Calm, calm, rolling the trains. Calm monumentally vacant. No more point. Keel carried along, keel rocked.

Unconscious of the earth . . .

. . . .

Cold draft under me, warm draft above.

Tired of climbing, am I going to come down? But I am no longer tired. I no longer know anything of tiredness. I am no longer acquainted with it.

I am tall. I am the tallest one of all. The only one perhaps completely tall.

Where are the beings?

J'entends un murmure, un murmure s'organise. Au loin on a ombre sur moi. Quelqu'un me tire où je ne veux pas aller. Quelqu'un me prend où je ne m'aime pas. Non, cela se détache. Libre à nouveau. Espace-cristal. J'y vogue.

Ai-je un témoin? Silence souverain. Y a-t-il un autre témoin?

Grand, j'aimerais aller vers plus grand encore, vers l'absolument grand. Je m'offre s'il existe. J'offre mon néant suspendu, ma soif jamais encore étanchée, ma soif jamais encore satisfaite.

Tout convient: Le lieu est vaste. Plus de fermeture. Pas de témoins.

Fais signe si tu existes, viens, me prenant comme insecte dans une couverture, viens tout de suite. Ceux d'en bas tirent sur moi, cerf-volant dans le vent, cerf-volant qui ne peut résister, qui ne peut couper sa corde.

Tu dois le voir.

Maintenant l'instant est passé (ou le siècle?)

Qu'est-il arrivé? Quelle rencontre?

Je ne suis plus pareil. Etre, ou substance ou j'ai pris bain?

Plus de doute, ils tirent d'en bas, me chargeant de lest, de lest de plus en plus.

Combien c'est de mauvais augure, ces voix que j'entends, ces connivences, cet effort commun à plusieurs actes, l'action méchante qui me reprend, sorte d'épervier

I hear a rumor, a rumor forms! From far off a shadow is over me. Someone is dragging me where I don't want to go. Someone is taking me where I don't like myself. No, it's letting go. Free again. Crystal-space. I'm sailing through it.

Do I have a witness? Sovereign silence. Is there another witness?

Tall, I would like to go towards something taller yet, towards the absolutely tall. I offer myself if it exists. I offer my suspended nothingness, my thirst never yet quenched, my thirst never yet satisfied.

Everything fits: The place is vast. No more obstructions. No witnesses.

Give a sign if you exist, come, taking me like a bug in a blanket, come right away. The ones down below are tugging at me, kite in the wind, kite unable to resist, unable to cut its cord.

You must see it.

Now the moment is past (or the century?).

What happened? What encounter?

I am no longer the same. Being, or substance or I took a bath?

No longer any doubt, they're tugging from below, loading me with ballast, more and more ballast.

How ominous, these voices I hear, these connivings, this effort common to several actions, this nasty operation of recovering me, a sort of net cast over me. They

jeté sur moi. Ils tiennent l'ancre du corps. Que n'était-il plutôt détruit. J'avais laissé ce malheureux. Ils le manœuvrent.

Je descends. Bon, j'arrive. Ne me bourrez pas de pierres si lourdes, si dures, vous avez gagné, je viens, j'ai tout perdu. Ma fusée retombe, le poids en moi, le poids à nouveau, à nouveau la terre aux pieds. Que viens-je encore faire sur terre?

Henri Michaux

hold the body's anchor. Why couldn't it be destroyed instead? I had left this unhappy person. They are maneuvering him.

I'm going down. All right, I'm coming. Don't ram me with such heavy, such hard stones, you won, I'm coming, I've lost everything. My rocket falls down, the weight in me, again the weight, again the ground at my feet. What am I doing on the earth again?

Henri Michaux
Translated by Dori Katz

De sentir toute cette beauté dispersée dans les musées vient le désespoir de ne pouvoir la garder en soi. Audehors, on aperçoit les grands arbres d'un jardin alors que vole un oiseau des pays tempérés. Parfois, on entend gronder l'orage, les tableaux lentement s'assombrissent. Pour les vieux gardiens, cela fait diversion, ils commentent le ciel. Par les rues, les gens se hâtent devant de vastes monuments qui les oppressent. La pluie fouette des verrières, l'ouragan brise des branches, cependant que le portrait d'une femme nue sourit dans son cadre d'or noir, s'éclaire d'une lumière indécise.

Jean Follain
(*Etendues*)

from Extensions

From being aware of all this beauty scattered in museums comes the despair of not being able to hold on to it. Outside, one sees the tall trees of a garden as a bird of temperate regions takes flight. Sometimes, one hears the storm grumble, the paintings slowly darken. It's a diversion for the old guards, they comment on the sky. In the streets, people hurry before vast monuments that oppress them. The rain is whipping the glass, the hurricane is breaking branches, while the portrait of a naked woman smiles in its gilded black frame, grows bright with an uncertain light.

Jean Follain
Translated by Dori Katz

Que distraitement le promeneur pousse du pied un caillou violâtre, il rumine d'incertaines pensées. Les bruits sont bien ceux de son adolescence. Il passe devant une bâtisse où les cris des bêtes, à cause du temps couvert, semblent des appels sans recours. Il va sans but, pas comme ce cultivateur qui s'avance, qu'il va devoir saluer. Aussi, pour l'éviter, s'engage-t-il dans un chemin de traverse. Les pierres y apparaissent d'une autre couleur, les haies moins élaguées, plus accueillantes; le ciel bientôt s'y éclaircit, ouvert à l'événement.

Jean Follain
(*Allées et venues*)

from Comings and Goings

Should the stroller absentmindedly kick at a purplish pebble, he is mulling over vague thoughts. The noises are indeed those of his adolescence. He passes in front of a shed from which the cries of animals, on account of the overcast sky, seem futile calls for help. He walks, aimless, not like this approaching farmer he'll have to greet. So, to avoid him, he takes a side road. Here the stones are of a different color, the hedgerows less well pruned, more friendly; soon the sky clears, open to the event.

Jean Follain
Translated by Dori Katz

Le bruit du vent ravive d'anciennes journées quand le pain et le vin et même le pain trempé dans le vin avaient un autre goût. Un temps considérable a fini par s'amonceler. Certains chiffres d'années n'évoquent plus rien. Comme sortie des âges, une petite fille apparaît à qui on a bandé les yeux pour jouer au colin-maillard. Entourée de plusieurs autres fillettes qui courent autour d'elle, elle essaie de deviner le nom de qui l'a touchée. Ayant eu le temps de tirer sur une natte ensoleillée, d'un tressage tout spécial, elle devine et pousse alors un unique cri de contentement qui n'aura jamais son pareil.

Jean Follain
(*Allées et venues*)

from Comings and Goings

The sound of the wind revives former days when bread and wine and even bread soaked in wine had a different taste. A considerable amount of time has finally piled up. Certain numerals for years no longer evoke a thing. As though emerging from history, a girl appears whose eyes have been bound to play blindman's-buff. Surrounded by several other little girls who run around her, she tries to guess the name of the one who touched her. Having had the time to pull at a sunny braid, tied in a very special way, she guesses and then lets out a single scream of happiness never to be equaled.

Jean Follain
Translated by Dori Katz

Tu as bien fait de partir, Arthur Rimbaud!

Tu as bien fait de partir, Arthur Rimbaud! Tes dix-huit ans réfractaires à l'amitié, à la malveillance, à la sottise des poètes de Paris ainsi qu'au ronronnement d'abeille stérile de ta famille ardennaise un peu folle, tu as bien fait de les éparpiller aux vents du large, de les jeter sous le couteau de leur précoce guillotine. Tu as eu raison d'abandonner le boulevard des paresseux, les estaminets des pisselyres, pour l'enfer des bêtes, pour le commerce des rusés et le bonjour des simples.

Cet élan absurde du corps et de l'âme, ce boulet de canon qui atteint sa cible en la faisant éclater, oui, c'est bien là la vie d'un homme! On ne peut pas, au sortir de l'enfance, indéfiniment étrangler son prochain. Si les volcans changent peu de place, leur lave parcourt le grand vide du monde et lui apporte des vertus qui chantent dans ses plaies.

Tu as bien fait de partir, Arthur Rimbaud! Nous sommes quelques-uns à croire sans preuve le bonheur possible avec toi.

René Char

You Did Well to Leave, Arthur Rimbaud!

You did well to leave, Arthur Rimbaud! Your eighteen years of defiance, to friends and enemies alike, and to the inanities of the poets of Paris, as to the droning of that sterile bee, your provincial and crackpot family, you did well to scatter them to the wide winds, to cast them under the knife of their upstart guillotine. You were right to abandon the streets of idlers, the tavern of lyric-pissers, for the hell of beasts, for the commerce of the crafty, and the greetings of simple men.

That absurd leap of body and soul, that cannonball that strikes its target in the act of bursting, yes, that, surely, is the life of a man! We cannot, emerging from childhood, strangle our neighbors indefinitely. What if volcanos barely stir, their lava scours the great emptiness of the world and brings it the virtues which sing in its wounds.

You did well to leave, Arthur Rimbaud! You need not prove to us, a few believers, the happiness possible with you.

René Char
Translated by Rosalind Sherk

Antonin Artaud

Je n'ai pas de voix pour faire ton éloge, grand frère.
Si je me penchais sur ton corps que la lumière va
éparpiller,
Ton rire me repousserait.
Le cœur entre nous, durant ce qu'on appelle improprement un bel orage,
Tombe plusieurs fois,
Tue, creuse et brûle,
Puis renaît plus tard dans la douceur du champignon.
Tu n'as pas besoin d'un mur de mots pour exhausser ta
vérité,
Ni des volutes de la mer pour oindre ta profondeur,
Ni de cette main fiévreuse qui vous entoure le poignet,
Et légèrement vous mène abattre une forêt
Dont nos entrailles sont la hache.
Il suffit. Rentre au volcan.
Et nous,
Que nous pleurions, assumions ta relève ou demandions:
"Qui est Artaud?" à cet épi de dynamite dont aucun
grain ne se détache,
Pour nous, rien n'est changé,
Rien, sinon cette chimère bien en vie de l'enfer qui
prend congé de notre angoisse.

René Char

Antonin Artaud

I do not have the voice to praise you, great brother.
If I bent over your body which the light is going to
scatter,
Your laugh would drive me back.
The heart shared by us, during what is improperly called
a fine storm,
Sinks several times,
Kills, goes hollow and burns,
Then is reborn in the softness of the mushroom.
You do not need a wall of words to elevate your truth,
Nor scrolls of the sea to anoint your depths,
Nor this feverish hand which encircles your wrist,
And leads you lightly to chop down a forest
With our entrails for an axe.
It suffices. Go back into the volcano.
And as for us,
Whether we weep, relieve you, or ask, of that dynamite ear
not one grain of which breaks off: "Who is Artaud?"
For us, nothing is changed,
Nothing, other than this very much alive chimera out of
hell which from our anguish takes its leave.

René Char
Translated by David Lunde

Quatre Fascinants

I

LE TAUREAU

Il ne fait jamais nuit quand tu meurs,
Cerné de ténèbres qui crient,
Soleil aux deux pointes semblables.

Fauve d'amour, vérité dans l'épée,
Couple qui se poignarde unique parmi tous.

II

LA TRUITE

Rives qui croulez en parure
Afin d'emplir tout le miroir,
Gravier où balbutie la barque
Que le courant presse et retrousse,
Herbe, herbe toujours étirée,
Herbe, herbe jamais en répit,
Que devient votre créature
Dans les orages transparents
Où son cœur la précipita?

Four Fascinators

I

THE BULL

It's never night when you die,
Ringed by shouting shadows,
Sun with two similar horns.

Wild beast of love, verity in the blade,
Couple which stab one another unique among all.

II

THE TROUT

Banks which crumble bejeweled
In order to fill the whole mirror,
Gravel where stammers the boat
Which the current hurries and turns up,
Grass, grass, always stretched,
Grass, grass, never at ease,
What becomes of your creature
In the transparent storms
Where her heart plunged her?

III

LE SERPENT

Prince des contre-sens, exerce mon amour
A tourner son Seigneur que je hais de n'avoir
Que trouble répression ou fastueux espoir.

Revanche à tes couleurs, débonnaire serpent,
Sous le couvert du bois et en toute maison.
Par le lien qui unit la lumière à la peur,
Tu fais semblant de fuir, ô serpent marginal!

IV

L'ALOUETTE

Extrême braise du ciel et première ardeur du jour,
Elle reste sertie dans l'aurore et chante la terre agitée,
Carillon maître de son haleine et libre de sa route.

Fascinante, on la tue en l'émerveillant.

René Char

III

THE SERPENT

Prince of misconstructions, train my love,
To circumvent its Lord whom I hate for having
Dim repression only or gaudy hope.

Revenge to your colors, kindly serpent,
Under the cover of woods and in every house.
By the bond which unites light to fear,
You pretend to flee, o marginal serpent.

IV

THE LARK

Last cinder of sky and first ardor of day,
She remains mounted in dawn and sings perturbed earth,
Carillon master of her breath and free of her route.

A fascinator, she's killed by being dazzled.

René Char
Translated by Richard G. Stern

Victoire éclair

L'oiseau bêche la terre,
Le serpent sème,
La mort améliorée
Applaudit la récolte.

Pluton dans le ciel!

L'explosion en nous.
Là seulement dans moi.
Fol et sourd, comment pourrais-je l'être davantage?

Plus de second soi-même, de visage changeant, plus de saison pour la flamme et de saison pour l'ombre!

Avec la lente neige descendent les lépreux.

Soudain l'amour, l'égal de la terreur,
D'une main jamais vue arrête l'incendie, redresse le soleil, reconstruit l'Amie.

Rien n'annonçait une existence si forte.

René Char

Lightning Victory

The bird spades the soil,
The serpent sows,
Death, mended,
Applauds the harvest.

Pluto in heaven!

The explosion inside us.
There, in me only.
Deaf and crazed, how could I be more so?

No more second selves, faces that change, no more
seasons of flame and seasons of shadow.

With the slow snow the lepers come down.

Suddenly love, the peer of terror,
With unseen hand arrests the fire, puts right the sun,
reconstructs the Loved One.

Nothing foretold an existence of such strength.

René Char
Translated by Dori Katz and Donald Justice

La Bibliothèque est en feu

A Georges Braque

Par la bouche de ce canon il neige. C'était l'enfer dans notre tête. Au même moment c'est le printemps au bout de nos doigts. C'est la foulée de nouveau permise, la terre en amour, les herbes exubérantes.

L'esprit aussi, comme toute chose, a tremblé.

L'aigle est au futur.

Toute action qui engage l'âme, quand bien même celle-ci en serait ignorante, aura pour épilogue un repentir ou un chagrin. Il faut y consentir.

Comment me vint l'écriture? Comme un duvet d'oiseau sur ma vitre, en hiver. Aussitôt s'éleva dans l'âtre une bataille de tisons qui n'a pas, encore à présent, pris fin.

Soyeuses villes du regard quotidien, insérées parmi d'autres villes, aux rues tracées par nous seuls, sous l'aile d'éclairs qui répondent à nos attentions.

Tout en nous ne devrait être qu'une fête joyeuse quand quelque chose que nous n'avons pas prévu, que nous n'éclairons pas, qui va parler à notre cœur, par ses seuls moyens, s'accomplit.

Continuons à jeter nos coups de sonde, à parler à voix égale, par mots groupés, nous finirons par faire taire

The Library Is on Fire

to Georges Braque

Snow is falling from the mouth of this cannon. There was hell in our heads. At the same time, spring's at our fingertips. Permission's granted to step forth again, the earth's in love, the grasses exuberant.

So, too, the spirit has trembled, like all things.

The eagle is in the future.

Every act which engages the entire self, even though the self may be unaware of it, will have, as its epilogue, either repentance or chagrin. One must accept it.

How did writing come to me? Like bird's down against my windowpane, in wintertime. Immediately, among the embers in the hearth, there flared up a struggle which has not even yet come to an end.

Silken towns of the everyday gaze, wedged in among other towns, with streets traced only by ourselves, under the wing of lightning-flashes that respond to our attentions.

Within us all things should be nothing else than a joyful celebration, whenever something unforeseen, something on which we can throw no light, which will speak to our heart, by its own means, comes to pass.

Let us go on casting our sounding-leads, speaking in an even voice, with words assembled together, we shall

tous ces chiens, par obtenir qu'ils se confondent avec l'herbage, nous surveillant d'un œil fumeux, tandis que le vent effacera leur dos.

L'éclair me dure.

Il n'y a que mon semblable, la compagne ou le compagnon, qui puisse m'éveiller de ma torpeur, déclencher la poésie, me lancer contre les limites du vieux désert afin que j'en triomphe. Aucun autre. Ni cieux, ni terre privilégiée, ni choses dont on tressaille.

Torche, je ne valse qu'avec lui.

On ne peut pas commencer un poème sans une parcelle d'erreur sur soi et sur le monde, sans une paille d'innocence aux premiers mots.

Dans le poème, chaque mot ou presque doit être employé dans son sens originel. Certains, se détachant, deviennent plurivalents. Il en est d'amnésiques. La constellation du Solitaire est tendue.

La poésie me volera ma mort.

Pourquoi *poème pulvérisé?* Parce qu'au terme de son voyage vers le Pays, après l'obscurité pré-natale et la dureté terrestre, la finitude du poème est lumière, apport de l'être à la vie.

Le poète ne retient pas ce qu'il découvre; l'ayant transcrit, le perd bientôt. En cela réside sa nouveauté, son infini et son péril.

end by quieting all those dogs, by getting them mixed in with the grass, watching us with a cloudy eye while the wind rubs out their backs.

With me lightning lasts.

It is only my fellowman—companion, male or female —who can rouse me from my torpor, release poetry, hurl me against the boundaries of the old desert so that I may triumph over it. No one else. Neither the heavens nor the privileged earth nor things that shake us.

A torch, I waltz only with him.

One cannot begin a poem without a portion of error about oneself and the world, without some mote of innocence in the first words.

In the poem, each, or almost each word, must be used in its original sense. Certain ones, breaking away, become polyvalent. Some are amnesic. The constellation of the Lonely One is stretched taut.

Poetry will rob me of my death.

Why "pulverized poem"? Because near the end of its journey towards that country, after the prenatal darkness and the earthly harshness, the finitude of the poem is light, a contribution of being to life.

The poet does not keep what he discovers; having transcribed it, soon loses it. Therein lie his novelty, his infinity, and his peril.

Mon métier est un métier de pointe.

On naît avec les hommes, on meurt inconsolé parmi les dieux.

La terre qui reçoit la graine est triste. La graine qui va tant risquer est heureuse.

Il est une malédiction qui ne ressemble à aucune autre. Elle papillote dans une sorte de paresse, a une nature avenante, se compose un visage aux traits rassurants. Mais quel ressort, passée la feinte, quelle course immédiate au but! Probablement, car l'ombre où elle échafaude est maligne, la région parfaitement secrète, elle se soustraira à une appellation, s'esquivera toujours à temps. Elle dessine dans le voile du ciel de quelques clairvoyants des paraboles assez effrayantes.

Livres sans mouvement. Mais livres qui s'introduisent avec souplesse dans nos jours, y poussent une plainte, ouvrent des bals.

Comment dire ma liberté, ma surprise, au terme de mille détours: il n'y a pas de fond, il n'y a pas de plafond.

Parfois la silhouette d'un jeune cheval, d'un enfant lointain, s'avance en éclaireur vers mon front et saute la barre de mon souci. Alors sous les arbres reparle la fontaine.

Nous désirons rester inconnus à la curiosité de celles qui nous aiment. Nous les aimons.

My craft is a craft of the spearhead.

One is born along with other men; one dies, unconsoled, among the gods.

The earth that receives the seed is sad. The seed that's going to risk so much is happy.

There's one curse that resembles no other. It blinks in a sort of indolence, has an engaging disposition, composes for itself a face with reassuring features. But what energy, once past pretense, what an immediate dash towards the goal! Probably, since the shadow in which it builds is sly, the region utterly secret, it will escape being named, will always slip away in time. In the veil of the sky of those few with clear sight it traces quite frightening parables.

Books without movement. But books which work their way pliantly into our days, utter a complaint there, open great dances.

How to express my freedom, my surprise, at the end of a thousand turnings: there is no bottom, there is no ceiling.

Sometimes the silhouette of a colt, of a faraway child, comes scouting towards my brow and leaps the bar of my concern. Then, under the trees, the fountain speaks again.

We want to remain strangers to the curiosity of those who love us. We love them.

La lumière a un âge. La nuit n'en a pas. Mais quel fut l'instant de cette source entière?

Ne pas avoir plusieurs morts suspendues et comme enneigées. N'en avoir qu'une, de bon sable. Et sans résurrection.

Arrêtons-nous près des êtres qui peuvent se couper de leurs ressources, bien qu'il n'existe pour eux que peu ou pas de repli. L'attente leur creuse une insomnie vertigineuse. La beauté leur pose un chapeau de fleurs.

Oiseaux qui confiez votre gracilité, votre sommeil périlleux à un ramas de roseaux, le froid venu, comme nous vous ressemblons!

J'admire les mains qui emplissent, et, pour apparier, pour joindre, le doigt qui refuse le dé.

Je m'avise parfois que le courant de notre existence est peu saisissable, puisque nous subissons non seulement sa faculté capricieuse, mais le facile mouvement des bras et des jambes qui nous ferait aller là où nous serions heureux d'aller, sur la rive convoitée, à la rencontre d'amours dont les différences nous enrichiraient, ce mouvement demeure inaccompli, vite déclinant en image, comme un parfum en boule sur notre pensée.

Désir, désir qui sait, nous ne tirons avantage de nos ténèbres qu'à partir de quelques souverainetés véritables assorties d'invisibles flammes, d'invisibles chaînes, qui, se révélant, pas après pas, nous font briller.

Light has an age. Night has none. But what was the moment of that whole springing forth?

Let there not be several deaths hanging over us and as it were snowed in. Let there be only one—of good sandy ground. And without resurrection.

Let us keep near those who can cut themselves off from their resources, even though there is little or no falling back for them. Waiting carves out for them a giddy insomnia. Beauty decks them out with a hat of flowers.

Birds trusting your slenderness, your perilous sleep to a bunch of reeds, once the cold comes, how we resemble you!

I admire the hands that fill and, for matching, for joining, the finger which refuses the thimble.

I sometimes tell myself that the current of our existence is scarcely to be grasped, since we suffer not only its capricious power but also the easy motion of arms and legs that would make us go where we would be glad to go, up on the coveted shore, to the meeting with loves whose differences would enrich us, this movement remains incomplete, swiftly declining into an image, like a perfume-ball over our mind.

Desire, knowing desire, we only make darkness count upon setting out from certain true sovereignties, fitted with invisible flames, with invisible chains, which, being disclosed, step by step, make us shine.

La beauté fait son lit sublime toute seule, étrangement bâtit sa renommée parmi les hommes, à côté d'eux mais à l'écart.

Semons les roseaux et cultivons la vigne sur les coteaux, au bord des plaies de notre esprit. Doigts cruels, mains précautionneuses, ce lieu facétieux est propice.

Celui qui invente, au contraire de celui qui découvre, n'ajoute aux choses, n'apporte aux êtres que des masques, des entre-deux, une bouillie de fer.

Enfin toute la vie, quand j'arrache la douceur de ta vérité amoureuse à ton profond!

Restez près du nuage. Veillez près de l'outil. Toute semence est détestée.

Bienfaisance des hommes certains matins stridents. Dans le fourmillement de l'air en délire, je monte, je m'enferme, insecte indévoré, suivi et poursuivant.

Face à ces eaux, de formes dures, où passent en bouquets éclatés toutes les fleurs de la montagne verte, les Heures épousent des dieux.

Frais soleil dont je suis la liane.

René Char

Beauty makes her sublime bed all by herself, builds up her fame curiously among men, beside them but apart.

Let us sow reeds and cultivate the vineyard on the slopes, at the edge of our spirit's wounds. Cruel fingers, careful hands, this jesting place is propitious.

He who invents, in contrast to him who discovers, adds to things only, supplies men only with masks, insertions, iron pulp.

All life, at last, when I draw the sweetness of your loving truth up from your depths!

Stay near the cloud. Keep watch near the tool. Every seed is hated.

Men's charity on certain shrill mornings. In the tingling of air in frenzy, I rise, I shut myself in, an undevoured insect, pursued and pursuing.

Facing these waters, hard in outline, where all the flowers of the green mountain pass by in exploding bouquets, the hours marry the gods.

Fresh sun, whose liana I am.

René Char
Translated by Ralph Freedman,
Donald Justice, and Paulène Aspel

A deux enfants

1

J'ai vu tes yeux bleus de vingt jours
Donner un frisson clair aux feuilles
De l'ormeau et du tamaris.

J'ai vu ton père se grandir
En t'élevant sur sa poitrine
Et ta mère se définir
En baisant tes joues d'algue douce.

Dans le berceau conciliant
Où tu rougis, petite aurore,
Elisabeth, je te découvre
Comme la rose des sous-bois.

Et je suis heureux de cela,
Moi qui marche sous la pluie fine.

2

Hélène,
Au lent berceau, au doux cheval,
Bonjour! Mon auberge est la tienne.

Comme ta chaleur est adroite
Qui sait, en biais, m'atteindre au cœur,
Enfant chérie des ruisseaux, des rêveurs,
Hélène! Hélène!

For Two Children

1

I saw your twenty-day blue eyes
Give a bright shudder to the leaves
Of the elm and tamarisk.

I saw your father grow taller
While lifting you to his chest
And your mother reveal herself
While kissing your seaweed-sweet cheeks.

In the reconciling cradle
Where you blush, little dawn,
Elizabeth, I discover you
Like the rose in the undergrowth.

And I am happy for that,
I walking under the fine rain.

2

Hélène
With your slow cradle, with your sweet horse,
Greetings! My inn is yours.

How clever your warmth is
Knowing obliquely how to reach my heart
Dear child of streams and dreams.
Hélène! Hélène!

René Char

Mais que te veulent les saisons
Qui t'aiment de quatre manières?
Que ta beauté, cette lumière
Entre et passe en chaque maison?
Ou, que la lune à jamais grande
Te tienne et t'entoure la main
Jusqu'à l'amour que tu demandes?

René Char

But what do the seasons want from you
Who love you in four ways?
That your beauty, like light,
Enter and dwell in each house?
Or that the always full moon
Surround your hand and take you
Up to the love you need?

René Char
Translated by Paul Engle

L'Eternité à Lourmarin

Albert Camus

Il n'y a plus de ligne droite ni de route éclairée avec un être qui nous a quittés. Où s'étourdit notre affection? Cerne après cerne, s'il approche c'est pour aussitôt s'enfouir. Son visage parfois vient s'appliquer contre le nôtre, ne produisant qu'un éclair glacé. Le jour qui allongeait le bonheur entre lui et nous n'est nulle part. Toutes les parties—presque excessives—d'une présence se sont d'un coup disloquées. Routine de notre vigilance . . . Pourtant cet être supprimé se tient dans quelque chose de rigide, de désert, d'essentiel en nous, où nos millénaires ensemble font juste l'épaisseur d'une paupière tirée.

Avec celui que nous aimons, nous avons cessé de parler, et ce n'est pas le silence. Qu'en est-il alors? Nous savons, ou croyons savoir. Mais seulement quand le passé qui signifie s'ouvre pour lui livrer passage. Le voici à notre hauteur, puis loin, devant.

A l'heure de nouveau contenue où nous questionnons tout le poids d'énigme, soudain commence la douleur, celle de compagnon à compagnon, que l'archer, cette fois, ne transperce pas.

René Char

Eternity at Lourmarin

Albert Camus

There is no longer a straight line nor a road brightened with a being who has left us. Where does our affection dazzle itself? Circle after circle, if he approaches it is to bury himself at once. Sometimes his face presses against ours, producing only a frozen light. The day which prolonged happiness between him and us is nowhere. All the parts—almost excessive—of a presence are suddenly dislocated. Routine of our vigilance . . . Yet this suppressed being survives in something rigid, barren, intrinsic in us, where our millennia together scarcely make the thickness of a drawn eyelid.

We have stopped speaking with the one we love, and it is not silence. What is it then? We know, or think we know. But only when the significant past opens to give him passage. He is here at our height, then far away, ahead.

In that once more held-in moment when we question all the weight of the enigma, suddenly begins that sadness from companion to companion which the archer, this time, cannot pierce.

René Char
Translated by Paul Engle

Contrevenir

Obéissez à vos porcs qui existent. Je me soumets à mes dieux qui n'existent pas.

Nous restons gens d'inclémence.

René Char

Contravention

Obey your swine which do exist. I submit myself to my gods who do not.

We remain inclement folk.

René Char
Translated by David Lunde

Le Lieu miraculeux de l'amour

Si intimement pareille à qui j'étais
révolté dans le malheur d'exil
Ton présent miroir encore de mes jours passés
et moi soudain loin d'eux pour me soustraire
aux déchirures dont ton amour m'a guéri
Nous avons aveuglé les miroirs
et nous nous découvrons dans la même buée
compagnons d'un pays où nous avons su nous perdre.

André Frénaud

The Miraculous Place of Love

So intimately like the one I used to be
a rebel in the misfortune of exile
Your present still a mirror of my past days
and I far from them suddenly to avoid
the rents which your love cured me of
We have made blind the mirrors
and we discover each other in the same mist
companions in a country where we knew how to lose
ourselves.

André Frénaud
Translated by Paulène Aspel

Pays retrouvé

Mon cœur moins désaccordé de tout ce qu'il aimait
je ne fais plus obstacle à ce pays bien-aimé
J'ai dépassé ma fureur j'ai découvert
le passé accueillant Aujourd'hui je peux j'ose

Je me fie au chemin j'épèle ici sans crainte
la montée les détours Un songe vrai s'étale
Je m'y retrouve dans le murmure qui ne cesse pas
Le vent rien que le vent me mène où je désire

Des paroles inconnues me parviennent familières
Des regards bienveillants me suivent dans les arbres
Je me reconnais ici j'avoue mon pays cette terre-ci
et toute contrée où des hameaux apparaissent
où des coqs flambent près de la tour
avec la verveine dans le potager les massifs entre les murs

Les rangées des vignes se tiennent sur les versants
et les nuages se promènent lentement dans l'azur
creusant d'ombre la plaine où les céréales jaunissent

Tout est beau qui s'entrouvre aujourd'hui où je passe
O je me souviendrai de ce vrai pain des hommes
Je veux goûter de ces raisins qui sèchent
pendus sous la galerie.

André Frénaud

Rediscovered Country

My heart less out of tune with all it loved
I object no more to this beloved country
I went beyond my anger I discovered
the welcoming past Today I can I dare

I trust the road I spell here without fear
the slope the windings A true dream unfolds
I find myself again in the unceasing whisper
The wind only the wind takes me where I please

Unheard of words reach me as known
Well-wishing looks follow me in the trees
Here I realize myself I confess this land my country
and any country where hamlets appear
where roosters are aflame beside the tower
with verbena in gardens groves between walls

Rows of vines are standing on hillsides
and clouds stroll slowly in the blue sky
shade furrowing the plain where crops turn yellow

All's beautiful that today half opens where I pass
O I shall remember this true bread of men
I want to taste these drying grapes
hung from the archways.

André Frénaud
Translated by Paulène Aspel

Qui possède quoi?

Qui possède quoi dans ces enclos? A qui est-ce
la montagne investie jusqu'au sommet,
les murs patients, les blés jaunes, les amandiers?
Serait-ce à toi, à toi, ce beau domaine,
la maison, la pièce d'eau précieuse,
l'enfant qui crie sur la pelouse?
Ah, qui saura retenir entre ses mains
les murs qui tombent, la fleur immuable,
les héritages démembrés, les puits taris?
Des familles éteintes qui lira les noms
sur la mousse des tombes oubliées?
Et le vent, les rochers, et la mort, à qui est-ce?

André Frénaud

Who Owns What?

Who owns what in these enclosures? Whose
the mountain besieged to the very top,
the patient walls, yellow wheat, almond trees?
Would this fine domain be yours, yours
the house, the precious pond,
the child who cries on the lawn?
Ah, who can keep in his hands
the crumbling walls, the immutable flower,
dismantled estates and dried up wells?
Who will read dead families' names
on the moss-grown forgotten graves?
And wind, and rocks, and death, whose are they?

André Frénaud
Translated by Paulène Aspel

Il y en a qui doivent
Parler, parler encore à l'ombre dans les coins

Des plaies qui cicatrisent avec beaucoup de mal
Dans la nuit la plus claire

Et des étangs qui bâillent
On dirait contre un mur
Qui les tiendrait couchés.

Il y en a qui doivent
Longer ce mur, le même,
Et tâcher de l'ouvrir

Avec des mots, des noms qu'il s'agit de trouver
Pour tout ce qui n'a pas de forme et pas de nom.

Guillevic
(*Elégies*)

from Elegies

There are some who must
Speak, speak on in the shadow in the corners

About wounds that mend with difficulty
On the clearest of nights

And of ponds, yawning,
It seems, in the face of a wall
That would hold them down.

There are some who must
Hug this wall, the same wall,
And try to force it open

With words, with names still to be found
For that which has no form and has no name.

Guillevic
Translated by Tod Perry
and Maurice O'Meara

Ils sont heureux
Ceux pour qui l'eau
Est la patrie.

Ils voient les lacs et les rivières
Et tout s'apaise
Dans la bénédiction des eaux.

Plus loin, plus bas, au fond de l'eau,
Est le secret qui les conduit,
Rêvant et soulevés
Par le vent de l'aval.

Ils s'assoient dans les joncs et voient que tout s'achève
Dans l'eau qui se souvient
D'avoir fini sa peine.

Guillevic
(*Elégies*)

from Elegies

Happy are they
For whom water
Is home.

They no sooner see the lakes and the rivers,
Than everything's composed
In the blessing of the waters.

Farther on, down, in the water's depth
Lies the secret that leads them
Dreaming and swept up
By the downward wind.

They sit among reeds and see everything come to rest
In the water that remembers
Having finished with its pain.

Guillevic
Translated by Tod Perry
and Maurice O'Meara

Midi c'est l'étranger
Qui se nourrit en vain
De l'étendue des prés
Et des furies d'insectes

Quand la patrie est dans les caves
Avec la bave des limaces.

Guillevic
(*Elégies*)

from Elegies

Noon is the outsider
Who feeds in vain
On the stretched-out fields
And on furies of insects

When home is in caves
With the drool of slugs.

Guillevic
Translated by Tod Perry
and Maurice O'Meara

Il aura trop tenu
Dans le fond de sa paume
En face de la mer

Du sable que le vent
Y prenait grain par grain

Celui que tient la peur
De devenir nuage.

Guillevic
(*Elégies*)

from Elegies

He probably held too tight,
In the hollow of his hand,
Looking out on the sea,

To the sand the wind
Was taking grain by grain—

He who harbors fear
Of becoming mist.

Guillevic
Translated by Tod Perry
and Maurice O'Meara

La Couleur du froid

Non pas le noir, car l'obscur est soie comme l'épouse dévêtue, et la grande nuit, qui rassemble tous les hommes sous un drapeau unique, est une mère prodigue de doux baumes, ni l'or du jour, car il participe du feu élémentaire, c'est le blanc qui est la couleur du froid. Sans doute (et par bonheur) que le blanc n'existe pas, puisque jamais on ne l'a vu qu'entaché de gris, qui n'est autre que bleu, vert ou noir encore. Mais le peintre (idéal) que je songe, il lui suffirait, frisant du doigt un bouc candide, roulant un œil rosé dans le triangle clair, d'une touche, la plus infime, de telle couleur idéalement pure, pour qu'à l'instant le froid absolu rayonne, destructeur de toute vie (que le peintre avait créée, selon les commentaires) sur un globe enfermé dans une gangue dure.

André Pieyre de Mandiargues

The Color of Cold

Not black (for darkness is silk like the bride undressed, and the wide night, which gathers everyone under one flag, is a mother prodigal of soft balms) nor the gold of day (for it partakes of the elemental fire), but white—white is the color of cold. Very likely (and fortunate it is) white does not exist, since never has it been seen unflecked with gray, which is nothing but blue, green, or, once again, black. But the (ideal) painter I imagine—curling with one finger his simple goatee, rolling one rosy eye up into the clear triangle—for him one touch, the most infinitesimal, of so ideally pure a color, would suffice for absolute cold on the instant to shine forth, destroyer of all life (which the painter had created, according to commentaries) upon a globe enclosed within a hard veinstone.

André Pieyre de Mandiargues
Translated by Donald Justice

Le Grand Théâtre

Tous les acteurs (et les actrices) ont fini le même jour, sur un décret du kan qu'ils fussent, après étranglement, momifiés à l'intérieur de leur propre effigie, de cire, peinte et vêtue, pour garder aux générations futures l'image du drame et de la comédie tels que ce siècle les aima. Le grand théâtre n'est plus ouvert qu'aux matins les plus froids de la saison, quand le mercure est d'un onglet de Chine au-dessous du zéro centigrade. Les maîtres ont respecté la salle, qui est tout ainsi que naguère, mais le toit fut aboli du côté de la scène, sans raison. Un air glacé, dès le lever du rideau, pénètre et tourbillonne. Aussi ne va-t-on qu'en pelisse, ganté de laine double, masqué de peau de chat, à l'orchestre ou au balcon, et les loges sont-elles à l'abandon, car l'habit noir et les épaules nues n'ont pas cessé d'y être de rigueur. L'on ne va plus au grand théâtre que pour voir tomber la neige dans le vide, sur fond de pourpre et d'or, et pour entendre le bruit de la neige qui bat doucement sur le velours.

André Pieyre de Mandiargues

The Big Theater

All the actors (and the actresses) ended the same day, on a decree of the Khan that they be, after strangulation, mummified inside their own wax effigies, painted and dressed, to preserve for future generations the picture of drama and comedy as this century loved them. The big theater is no longer open except on the coldest mornings of the season, when the mercury is a Chinese notch below zero centigrade. The masters have respected the hall: it is precisely as before, except for the roof near the stage which has been destroyed, without reason. A frigid air, when the curtain rises, penetrates and whirls about. So, one goes in furs, in double-lined wool gloves, trimmed in cat's fur, to the orchestra, or to the balcony: the loges have been abandoned, for formal dress, black tie, and bare shoulders are still required. One goes now to the big theater only to see the snow falling into the space there, against a background of purple and gold, and to hear the sound of that snow beating gently upon velvet.

André Pieyre de Mandiargues
Translated by Charles P. Wright, Jr.

Haut Lieu

Souvent le soir est rouge
Quand des traînées de sang passent à vau de ciel
Sur le pointu des toits de la Cité

La nuit se teint de rouge
Quand je pense à René Crevel
Qui fut comme un pavé de Paris
Jeté au front des lis

Il est un grand poing rouge
Feu (silence)
Sous l'arche des ponts
Au-dessus de l'eau noire

Les hommes qui ont cru purement en toi
Révolution
Sont morts

Tour encore
Plus haut que nul poing ou feu
Que l'on ait pu voir dans les nuits
Tu es dressée
Pourtant

Et tu portes des noms ainsi que des têtes

L'un de ces noms mis en haut lieu
Est celui de René Crevel

André Pieyre de Mandiargues

High Place

Often the evening is red
Whenever trails of blood slip down the sky
Onto the pointed roofs of the City

Night is tinted with red
Whenever I think of René Crevel
Who was like one of the cobblestones of Paris
Flung in the lilies' face

He is a great red fist
Fire (silence)
Below the arch of the bridges
Over black water

The men who believed in you purely
Revolution
Are dead

Still a tower
Higher than any fist or fire
That has ever been seen by night
You are standing
Even so

And you bear names as well as heads

One of those names set in a high place
Is that of René Crevel

André Pieyre de Mandiargues
Translated by Donald Justice

Poème d'amour à Hélène

Comme un fleuve s'est mis
A aimer son voyage
Un jour tu t'es trouvée
Dévêtue dans mes bras

Et je n'ai plus songé
Qu'à te couvrir de feuilles
De mains nues et de feuilles
Pour que tu n'aies point froid

Car t'aimais-je autrement
Qu'à travers tes eaux vives
Corps de femme un instant
Suspendu à mes doigts

Et pouvais-je poser
Sur tant de pierres chaudes
Un regard qui n'aurait
Eté que du désir?

Vierge tu réponds mieux
A l'obscure sentence
Que mon cœur fait peser
Doucement sur ton cœur

Love Poem to Helen

Like a river that's begun
To love its journey
You found yourself one day
Naked in my arms

And I had no thought
But to cover you with leaves,
With bare hands and leaves,
So you would not be cold.

For could I love you less
Than through your lively waters,
Body of woman balanced
A moment on my fingers,

And could I let a glance
Touch such hot stones
That would have been a glance
Merely of desire?

Virgin you answer more
To the dark sentence
That my heart presses
Gently on your heart

Et si j'ai le tourment
De ta métamorphose
C'est qu'il me faut aimer
Ton amour avant toi.

René Guy Cadou

And if I find torment
In your metamorphosis,
It's this: that I must love
Your love before you.

René Guy Cadou
Translated by
Edmund Keeley

Celui qui entre par hasard

Celui qui entre par hasard dans la demeure d'un poète
Ne sait pas que les meubles ont pouvoir sur lui
Que chaque nœud du bois renferme davantage
De cris d'oiseaux que tout le cœur de la forêt
Il suffit qu'une lampe pose son cou de femme
A la tombée du soir contre un angle verni
Pour délivrer soudain mille peuples d'abeilles
Et l'odeur de pain frais des cerisiers fleuris
Car tel est le bonheur de cette solitude
Qu'une caresse toute plate de la main
Redonne à ces grands meubles noirs et taciturnes
La légèreté d'un arbre dans le matin.

René Guy Cadou

Who Risks It Where a Poet Lives

Who risks it where a poet lives
Forgets how things hold power there—
The wood holds coiled in every knot
More birdcalls than all the forest's heart,
A lamp can curve its girlish neck
Near nightfall by a gleaming wall
And spring a thousand hosts of bees
And the bakery smell from flowering cherries—
For it's the power of this lonely place
That at a slide of your open hand
Dark silent things relive, take on
The leap of a tree poised at dawn.

René Guy Cadou
Translated by William Stafford

Vrai Nom

Je nommerai désert ce château que tu fus,
Nuit cette voix, absence ton visage,
Et quand tu tomberas dans la terre stérile
Je nommerai néant l'éclair qui t'a porté.

Mourir est un pays que tu aimais. Je viens
Mais éternellement par tes sombres chemins.
Je détruis ton désir, ta forme, ta mémoire,
Je suis ton ennemi qui n'aura de pitié.

Je te nommerai guerre et je prendrai
Sur toi les libertés de la guerre et j'aurai
Dans mes mains ton visage obscur et traversé,
Dans mon cœur ce pays qu'illumine l'orage.

Yves Bonnefoy

True Name

Desert, I'll call this castle which you were;
Night, I'll name this voice; Absence this face;
And when you fall into the sterile earth,
That lightning which bore you here, Nothingness.

To die is a land you loved. I come
Only eternally by your dark ways.
I destroy your memory, desire, your form.
I am your foe who shall be pitiless.

I'll name you War and I shall take all fierce
Liberties of the war on you; I shall possess
Within my hands, your face, darkened and pierced,
Within my heart, this land, brightened by storm.

Yves Bonnefoy
Translated by W. D. Snodgrass

Menaces du témoin

I

Que voulais-tu dresser sur cette table,
Sinon le double feu de notre mort?
J'ai eu peur, j'ai détruit dans ce monde la table
Rougeâtre et nue, où se déclare le vent mort.

Puis j'ai vieilli. Dehors, vérité de parole
Et vérité de vent ont cessé leur combat.
Le feu s'est retiré qui était mon église,
Je n'ai même plus peur, je ne dors pas.

II

Vois, déjà tous chemins que tu suivais se ferment,
Il ne t'est plus donné même ce répit
D'aller même perdu. Terre qui se dérobe
Est le bruit de tes pas qui ne progressent plus.

Pourquoi as-tu laissé les ronces recouvrir
Un haut silence où tu étais venu?
Le feu veille désert au jardin de mémoire
Et toi, ombre dans l'ombre, où est-tu, qui es-tu?

III

Tu cesses de venir dans ce jardin,
Les chemins de souffrir et d'être seul s'effacent,
Les herbes signifient ton visage mort.

Threats of the Witness

I

What did you want to set out on that table
If not our death's twin fires? I was afraid,
And in this world destroyed the red and naked table
Where the dead wind defends its argument.

Then I grew old. Outside, the truth of wind
And the truth of speech in single combat keep
A sudden peace. The fiery church has drawn away,
And even fear has gone, I do not sleep.

II

All of the ways you took are overgrown,
You're no more granted even this relief
Of wandering lost even. The earth escapes me with
The sound of your footsteps that will go no farther.

Why did you leave the high silence where you'd come
To brambles? The fire, lone watchman, wanders through
The dry, nocturnal park of memory,
And you, shadow in shadow, where are you, who are you?

III

You will not come to this green place again,
The paths of suffering have vanished where you took
Your solitude, the grasses are your lifeless face.

Il ne t'importe plus que soient cachés
Dans la pierre l'église obscure, dans les arbres
Le visage aveuglé d'un plus rouge soleil,

Il te suffit
De mourir longuement comme en sommeil,
Tu n'aimes même plus l'ombre que tu épouses.

IV

Tu es seul maintenant malgré ces étoiles,
Le centre est près de toi et loin de toi,
Tu as marché, tu peux marcher, plus rien ne change,
Toujours la même nuit qui ne s'achève pas.

Et vois, tu es déjà séparé de toi-même,
Toujours ce même cri, mais tu ne l'entends pas,
Es-tu celui qui meurt, toi qui n'as plus d'angoisse,
Es-tu même perdu, toi qui ne cherches pas?

V

Le vent se tait, seigneur de la plus vieille plainte,
Serai-je le dernier qui s'arme pour les morts?
Déjà le feu n'est plus que mémoire et que cendre
Et bruit d'aile fermée, bruit de visage mort.

It cannot matter now that in the stone
The secret church still hides, or that the sun,
A blinded face, glows redder through the branches now.

It is enough for you
That dying is as long as sleep, and now
You can no longer love the shadow you have wed.

IV

You are alone, dark in the constant light
Of stars, the center is near and far away,
You have walked, you can walk, now nothing changes,
Always the same unconsummated night.

And see, already taken from yourself
You hear no longer that unchanging call,
Are you the one who dies, you who can feel your pain
No more, are you lost, you who do not search at all?

V

The wind keeps still, lord of the oldest complaint,
Am I the last defender for the race
Of dead men? The fire's a memory, an ash,
A whisper of folded wings and of a lifeless face.

Consens-tu de n'aimer que le fer d'une eau grise
Quand l'ange de ta nuit viendra clore le port
Et qu'il perdra dans l'eau immobile du port
Les dernières lueurs dans l'aile morte prises?

Oh, souffre seulement de ma dure parole
Et pour toi je vaincrai le sommeil et la mort,
Pour toi j'appellerai dans l'arbre qui se brise
La flamme qui sera le navire et le port.

Pour toi j'élèverai le feu sans lieu ni heure,
Un vent cherchant le feu, les cimes du bois mort,
L'horizon d'une voix ou les étoiles tombent
Et la lune mêlée au désordre des morts.

Yves Bonnefoy

Are you content to love the steel-gray tide
When your nocturnal angel, entering
To close the harbor, loses there the last
Glimmer reflected in his dying wing?

Endure only the hardness of my word,
And I will conquer death and sleep for you,
And call up in the shattered tree the flame
That will, for you, be ship and harbor too,

And out of time, and out of place will raise
A fire, a wind in search of fire, the dead
Tops of the woods, the sound of falling stars,
The moon in the disorder of the dead.

Yves Bonnefoy
Translated by William Brown

A San Francesco, le soir

. . . Ainsi le sol était de marbre dans la salle
Obscure, où te mena l'inguérissable espoir.
On eût dit d'une eau calme où de doubles lumières
Portaient au loin les voix des cierges et du soir.

Et pourtant nul vaisseau n'y demandait rivage,
Nul pas n'y troublait plus la quiétude de l'eau.
Ainsi, te dis-je, ainsi de nos autres mirages,
O fastes dans nos cœurs, ô durables flambeaux!

Yves Bonnefoy

San Francesco, at Night

And so, in that dark chamber, marble was the floor
On which you came, led on by Hope beyond all cure;
It might have been calm waters where redoubled lights
Bore far away the voice of candles and the night.

Yet, though, there was no ship there calling for a shore;
No footsteps troubled the water's stillness now. And so
It is, I tell you, it is so with our other mirages. O
Festivals of our heart, O torches which endure!

Yves Bonnefoy
Translated by W. D. Snodgrass

Art de la poésie

Dragué fut le regard hors de cette nuit.
Immobilisées et séchées les mains.
On a reconcilié la fièvre. On a dit au cœur
D'être le cœur. Il y avait un démon dans ces veines
Qui s'est enfui en criant.
Il y avait dans la bouche une voix morne sanglante
Qui a été lavée et rappelée.

Yves Bonnefoy

The Art of Poetry

Dredged out of that night were the eyes.
Fixed and dried up the hands.
The fever was reconciled. The heart was told
To be the heart. There was a demon in those veins
Which fled howling.
There was in the mouth a dejected and bleeding voice
Which was bathed and restored.

Yves Bonnefoy
Translated by Vincent Stewart

VI

Je marche, réuni au feu, dans le papier vague confondu avec l'air, la terre désamorcée. Je prête mon bras au vent.

Je ne vais pas plus loin que mon papier. Très loin au-devant de moi, il comble un ravin. Un peu plus loin dans le champ, nous sommes presque à égalité. A mi-genoux dans les pierres.

A côté, on parle de plaie, on parle d'un arbre. Je me reconnais. Pour ne pas être fou. Pour que mes yeux ne deviennent pas aussi faibles que la terre.

X

Je freine pour apercevoir le champ vide, le ciel au-dessus du mur. Entre l'air et la pierre, j'entre dans un champ sans mur. Je sens la peau de l'air, et pourtant nous demeurons séparés.

Hors de nous, il n'y a pas de feu.

André du Bouchet
(*Le Moteur blanc*)

from White Motor

VI

I walk, reunited with fire, in the uncertain paper blending with air, the unprimed earth. I lend my arm to the wind.

I go no farther than my paper. Very far ahead of me, it fills up a ravine. A little farther in the field, we are almost at a level. Half up to my knees in stones.

Nearby someone speaks of wounds, someone speaks of a tree. I know myself. That I not be mad. That my eyes not become as weak as earth.

X

I brake to see the vacant field, the sky above the wall. Between air and stone, I enter an unwalled field. I feel the air's skin and yet we remain divided.
Outside ourselves there is no fire.

André du Bouchet
Translated by Dori Katz

En pleine terre

En pleine terre
    les portes labourées portant air
  et fruits
ressac
blé d'orage
sec
le moyeu brûle
Je dois lutter contre mon propre bruit
la force de la plaine
que je brasse
et qui grandit
tout à coup un arbre rit
comme la route que mes pas
        enflamment
comme le couchant durement
        branché
comme le moteur rouge du vent
que j'ai mis à nu.

André du Bouchet

On the Open Earth

On the open earth
        the ploughed gates carrying air
    and fruit
surf
wheat from storms
dry
the hub burns
I must struggle against my own noise
the force of the plain
I stir up
and which grows
all at once a tree laughs
like the road my steps
        inflame
like the sunset harshly
        connected
like the red motor of the wind
I laid bare.

André du Bouchet
Translated by Warren Carrier

Le Vin du jour

Le vin du jour me gagne
au milieu du jour

le milieu rouge

avec une route au fond
et le roulement de la ferraille
qui m'appartient

la vaisselle
de la terre
croule

comme une maison

sous les pas

et je m'arrête
chaque fois qu'elle sonne
sur la prunelle des pierres.

André du Bouchet

The Wine of Day

The wine of day overtakes me
in the middle of the day

the red middle

with a road in the distance
and the rolling of scrap iron
that belongs to me

the crockery
of the earth
crumbles

like a house

under my feet

and I stop
each time it strikes
on the eye of the rocks.

André du Bouchet
Translated by
Warren Carrier

Cession

Le vent,
dans les terres sans eau de l'été, nous
quitte sur une lame,
ce qui subsiste du ciel.

En plusieurs fractures, la terre se précise. La
terre demeure stable dans le souffle qui nous
dénude.

Ici, dans le monde immobile et bleu, j'ai presque
atteint ce mur. Le fond du jour est encore devant
nous. Le fond embrasé de la terre. Le fond
et la surface du front,
aplani par le même souffle,
ce froid.

Je me recompose au pied de la façade comme l'air
bleu au pied des labours.

Rien ne désaltère mon pas.

André du Bouchet

Surrender

The wind,
in the waterless grounds of summer,
leaves us on a blade,
what remains of the sky.

Through several fractures, the earth defines itself. The earth remains stable in the breath that strips us.

Here, in the motionless blue world, I've almost reached that wall. The depths of the day are still before us. The blazing depths of the earth. The depths and
the surface of the face,
smoothed out by the same breath,
this coldness.

I compose myself anew at the base of the façade like the blue air at the edge of worked fields.

Nothing quenches my step.

André du Bouchet
Translated by Dori Katz

Sois tranquille, cela viendra! Tu te rapproches,
tu brûles! Car le mot qui sera à la fin
du poème, plus que le premier sera proche
de ta mort, qui ne s'arrête pas en chemin.

Ne crois pas qu'elle aille s'endormir sous des branches
ou reprendre souffle pendant que tu écris.
Même quand tu bois à la bouche qui étanche
la pire soif, la douce bouche avec ses cris

doux, même quand tu serres avec force le nœud
de vos quatre bras pour être bien immobiles
dans la brûlante obscurité de vos cheveux,

elle vient, Dieu sait par quels détours, vers vous deux,
de très loin ou déjà tout près, mais sois tranquille,
elle vient: d'un à l'autre mot tu es plus vieux.

Philippe Jaccottet
(*Quelques Sonnets*)

Sonnet

Don't worry, it will come! You're drawing near,
you're getting warm! For the word which is to end
the poem more than the first word will be near
your death, which won't be stopping along the way.

Don't think that it will doze off under the branches,
or pause to catch its breath while you are writing.
Even when you drink of the mouth which quenches
the deepest thirst, that soft mouth with its sweet

cries, even when you so make fast the knot
of your four arms that you can move no more
caught in the smoldering darkness of your hair,

it's coming, God knows how, towards both of you,
far off or here already, but don't worry,
it's coming: from one word to the next you age.

Philippe Jaccottet
Translated by Donald Justice

Intérieur

Il y a longtemps que je cherche à vivre ici,
dans cette chambre que je fais semblant d'aimer,
la table, les objets sans soucis, la fenêtre
ouvrant au bout de chaque nuit d'autres verdures,
et le cœur du merle bat dans le lierre sombre,
partout des lueurs achèvent l'ombre vieillie.

J'accepte moi aussi de croire qu'il fait doux,
que je suis chez moi, que la journée sera bonne.
Il y a juste, au pied du lit, cette araignée
(à cause du jardin), je ne l'ai pas assez
piétinée, on dirait qu'elle travaille encore
au piège qui attend mon fragile fantôme . . .

Philippe Jaccottet

Interior

This is where I have been trying to lead a life,
in this room of mine, I pretend to love
its table, all the neutral things, a window
forcing each darkness into a greener view.
The blackbird stirs a heart-beat in the thick ivy,
the first light sweeps at the retreating shadows.

I too am ready with this sweet acceptance,
that I belong here, that today brings promise.
But for this spider at the foot of my bed,
(from the garden, I suppose) which still weaves,
it seems—I did not crush it enough—
the web enshrouding my transparent self.

Philippe Jaccottet
Translated by David Pryce-Jones

La Traversée

Ce n'est pas la Beauté que j'ai trouvée ici,
ayant loué cette cabine de seconde,
débarqué à Palerme, oublié mes soucis,
mais celle qui s'enfuit, la beauté de ce monde.

L'autre, je l'ai peut-être vue en ton visage,
mais notre cours aura ressemblé à ces eaux
qui tracent leurs grands hiéroglyphes sur les plages
au sud de Naples, et que l'été boit aussitôt,

signes légers que l'on récrit sur les portières . . .
Elle n'est pas donnée à nous qui la forçons,
pareils à des aventuriers sur les frontières,
à des avares qui ont peur de la rançon.

Elle n'est pas non plus donnée aux lieux étranges,
mais peut-être à l'attente, au silence discret,
à celui qui est oublié dans les louanges
et simplement accroît son amour en secret.

Philippe Jaccottet

The Crossing

It is not Beauty I've discovered here—
having reserved this cabin, second-class,
landed at Palermo, forgot my care—
but the world's beauty only, which will pass.

I may have seen that other in your face,
but we are like these waters moving on,
that on the beaches south of Naples trace
great hieroglyphs, and are by summer gone,

faint signs, inscribed again on portières . . .
She is not given us who force our way,
who would adventure out on her frontiers,
misers, who fear the ransom we must pay.

She is not given to any foreign place,
although to waiting and to silence she may be,
to one forgotten in the midst of praise,
who simply tends his love, and secretly.

Philippe Jaccottet
Translated by Donald Justice

Le Travail du poète

L'ouvrage d'un regard d'heure en heure affaibli
n'est pas plus de rêver que de former des pleurs,
mais de veiller comme un berger et d'appeler
tout ce qui risque de se perdre s'il s'endort.

•

Ainsi, contre le mur éclairé par l'été
(mais ne serait-ce pas plutôt par sa mémoire),
dans la tranquillité du jour je vous regarde,
vous qui vous éloignez toujours plus, qui fuyez,
je vous appelle, qui brillez dans l'herbe obscure
comme autrefois dans le jardin, voix ou lueurs
(nul ne le sait) liant les défunts à l'enfance . . .
(Est-elle morte, telle dame sous le buis,
sa lampe éteinte, son bagage dispersé?
Ou bien va-t-elle revenir de sous la terre
et moi j'irais au-devant d'elle et je dirais:
"Qu'avez-vous fait de tout ce temps qu'on entendait
ni votre rire ni vos pas dans la ruelle?
Fallait-il s'absenter sans personne avertir?
O dame! revenez maintenant parmi nous . . .")

•

The Poet's Work

The work of a look hourly weakened
is no more to dream than to form tears,
but to watch like a shepherd and to call
everything that risks being lost if he nods.

•

Thus, against the wall lit-up by summer
(would it not rather be by its memory),
in the day's tranquillity I watch you,
you who continually retreat, escape,
I call you who shine in the dark grass
as once in the garden, voices or glimmers
(no one knows which), tying the dead to childhood . . .
(Is she dead, that lady under the boxwood,
her lamp extinguished, baggage scattered?
Or is she going to come back from underground,
and I, I'd go up to her and say,
"What have you done with all that time neither
your laughter nor your steps were heard in the lane?
Was it necessary to leave without warning anyone?
O lady! come back to us now . . .")

•

Dans l'ombre et l'heure d'aujourd'hui se tient cachée,
ne disant mot, cette ombre d'hier. Tel est le monde.
Nous ne le voyons pas très longtemps: juste assez
pour en garder ce qui scintille et va s'éteindre,
pour appeler encore et encore, et trembler
de ne plus voir. Ainsi s'applique l'appauvri,
comme un homme à genoux qu'on verrait s'efforcer
contre le vent de rassembler son maigre feu . . .

Philippe Jaccottet

Still hiding in today's hour and shadow,
saying nothing, yesterday's shadow. That's the world.
We don't see it very long, just enough
to keep what shines and is going to die down,
to call over and over, to tremble
at no longer seeing. Thus works the man grown poor,
like a man on his knees trying
to light a small fire against the wind . . .

Philippe Jaccottet
Translated by Richard G. Stern

Le Locataire

Nous habitons une maison légère haut dans les airs,
le vent et la lumière la cloisonnent en se croisant,
parfois tout est si clair que nous en oublions les ans,
nous volons dans un ciel à chaque porte plus ouvert.

Les arbres sont en bas, l'herbe plus bas, le monde vert,
scintillant le matin et, quand vient la nuit, s'éteignant,
et les montagnes qui respirent dans l'éloignement
sont si minces que le regard errant passe au travers.

La lumière est bâtie sur un abîme, elle est tremblante,
hâtons-nous donc de demeurer dans ce vibrant séjour,
car elle s'enténèbre de poussière en peu de jours
ou bien elle se brise et tout à coup nous ensanglante.

Porte le locataire dans la terre, toi, servante!
Il a les yeux fermés, nous l'avons trouvé dans la cour,
si tu lui as donné entre deux portes ton amour,
descends-le maintenant dans l'humide maison des
plantes.

Philippe Jaccottet

The Tenant

We live in a house light and high in air,
the walls are made of radiance crossing wind,
sometimes all is so clear years slip the mind,
we fly in a sky wider at every door.

Trees are below, grass lower, the green world,
sparkling at morning, fading at fall of night,
and distant breathing mountains are so slight
that by a passing glance they can be scaled.

The light is built on an abyss, and totters,
let's hurry then to hold this vibrant place,
for it will dim with dust in a few days
or bloody us when all at once it shatters.

You, housemaid, bear the tenant earthward hence!
His eyes are closed, we found him in the yard,
if you between two doors gave him your heart,
now draw him down to the damp house of plants.

Philippe Jaccottet
Translated by Harry Duncan

Le Règne minéral

Dans ce pays la foudre fait germer la pierre.

Sur les pitons qui commandent les gorges
Des tours ruinées se dressent
Comme autant de torches mentales actives
Qui raniment les nuits de grand vent
L'instinct de mort dans le sang du carrier.

Toutes les veines du granit
Vont se dénouer dans ses yeux.

Le feu jamais ne guérira de nous,
Le feu qui parle notre langue.

Jacques Dupin

The Mineral Kingdom

In this country the lightning makes stone spring up and
grow.

On the peaks commanding the gorges
Rise the ruined towers
Like so many active torches of the mind
That revive on the nights of great wind
The instinct of death in the blood of the quarryman.

All the veins of granite
Will unravel in his eyes.

The fire will never be cured of us,
The fire that speaks our language.

Jacques Dupin
Translated by William Brown

Le Partage

Une larme de toi fait monter la colonne du chant.
Une larme la ruine, et toute lumière est inhabitée.

La corde que je tresse, la rose que j'expie,
N'ont pas à redouter de lumière plus droite.

Le peu d'obscurité que je dilapide en montant
C'est de l'air qui me manque à l'approche des cimes.

Par le versant abrupt, la plus libre des routes,
Malgré le timon de la foudre et mes vomissements.

Jacques Dupin

The Portion

Your tear raises the column of song.
Your tear destroys it and all light is uninhabited.

The cord that I weave, the rose that I atone for,
Need not fear any more upstanding light.

The little obscurity that I squander in climbing
Is the air that fails me as I approach the peak.

By the abrupt slope, the freest of routes,
Despite the stroke of lightning, and my vomiting.

Jacques Dupin
Translated by Vincent Stewart

L'Air

Le corps et la rêverie de la dame
Pour qui tournoyaient les marteaux
Se perdent ensemble et reviennent,
Ne rapportant de la nuée
Que les guenilles de la foudre
Avec la future rosée.

Jacques Dupin

Air

The body and the dreams of the lady
For whom the hammers whirled
Are lost together, and return
Retrieving from the storm clouds
Only the tattered rags of the lightning
With the dew to come.

Jacques Dupin
Translated by William Brown

Ta nuque, plus bas que la pierre,
Ton corps plus nu
Que cette table de granit . . .

Sans le tonnerre d'un seul de tes cils,
Serais-tu devenue la même
Lisse et insaisissable ennemie
Dans la poussière de la route
Et la mémoire du glacier?

Amours anfractueuses, revenez,
Déchirez le corps clairvoyant.

Jacques Dupin
(*Saccades*)

from Fits and Starts

The back of your neck, more base than stone,
Your body more naked
Than this granite table . . .

Without the thunder from one of your eyelashes,
Would you have become the same
Smooth and ungraspable enemy
In the dust of the road
And the memory of the glacier?

Return, anfractuous loves,
Rend the clear-sighted body.

Jacques Dupin
Translated by James Stephens
and Wai-lim Yip

Selective Bibliography*

By Alexander Aspel

Pierre Reverdy

Born in 1889 at Narbonne in the south of France in a family of artisans. Settled in Paris as a proofreader for a newspaper in 1910. Friend of Apollinaire, Max Jacob, and cubist painters. Enlisted in the army during World War I. In 1917, after his medical discharge, published *Nord-Sud,* a review of modern art, in Paris. In 1926 returned to Catholicism and settled near the Abbaye de Solesmes. Died in 1960.

MAIN WORKS

Poèmes en prose. Paris: Editions P. Birault, 1915.

Epaves du ciel, poèmes 1915–1922. Paris: Editions Gallimard, 1924.

Le Gant de crin, notes. Paris: les petits-fils de Plon et Nourrit, 1926.

La Balle au bond, poèmes en prose. Paris: Cahiers du Sud, 1927.

Plupart du temps, poèmes, 1915–1922. Paris: Editions Gallimard, 1945.

Sources du vent. Paris-Genève: Editions des Trois Collines, 1946.

Le chant des morts. Paris: Tériade, 1948.

*Texts translated are given with French or/and English titles as they appear in their respective publications. The titles of the original works from which they were taken are given whenever indicated in the publication. (A.A.)

Le Livre de mon bord, notes 1930–1936. Paris: Mercure de France, 1948.

Main d'œuvre, poèmes 1913–1949. Paris: Mercure de France, 1949.

En vrac. Monaco: Editions du Rocher, 1956.

TO CONSULT

Cornell, K.: "The Case for Pierre Reverdy," *Essays in Honor of Albert Feuillerat.* New Haven: Yale University Press, 1943.

Emmanuel, P.: "De Mallarmé à Reverdy," *Poésie raison ardente.* Paris: Editions du Seuil, 1947.

Rousselot, J., and Manoll, M.: *Pierre Reverdy.* Paris: Seghers, 1951.

Béguin, A.: "Pierre Reverdy," *Poésie de la présence.* Paris: Editions du Seuil, 1957.

Grossvogel, D.: "Pierre Reverdy: The Fabric of Reality," *Yale French Studies,* no. 21, 1958.

Hommage à Pierre Reverdy, témoignages, textes, documents, correspondance inédite. Rodez: Subervie, 1961.

"Pierre Reverdy," *Mercure de France,* numéro spécial, janvier 1962.

Balakian, A.: "Pierre Reverdy and the Materio-Mysticism of Our Age," *American Society of Legion of Honor Magazine,* XXXIII, 1962.

Daniel, M.: "The Poetry of Pierre Reverdy," *Modern Language Review,* LVII, April 1963.

TRANSLATIONS

Conscience, tr.: J. Shipley. *Modern French Poetry,* editor and translator, J. Shipley. Greenberg, 1926.

The Line of Names and Faces / False Name / Grimace, tr.: not given. *New Directions in Prose and Poetry,* 1940.

Four Poems from *La Lucarne ovale* (1916): Monotonous Day / Motionless Reality / For the Moment / From Another Sky, tr.: Robert G. Cohn. *Yale French Studies,* no. 2, 1948.

Inn, tr.: Eugene Jolas. *Transition Workshop.* New York: The Vanguard Press, 1949.

Late Living / Unlucky Dawn / In a Lower Voice / My Dark Room / The Mind Emerges / Saltimbanques, tr.: William J. Smith. *Wake,* VI, 1953.

Secret, tr.: Charles Guenther. *University of Kansas City Review,* Winter 1954.

Memory / The Same Number / Miracle / False Door or Portrait / Late at Night / The Dry Tongue / Secret / The World before Me, tr.: Kenneth Rexroth. *New Directions in Prose and Poetry,* 1955.

Au-delà / Galeries / Quai aux fleurs / Spectacle des yeux / Chauffage central / L'Homme sacrifié / Les Battements du coeur / Arc-en-ciel / Figure délayée dans l'eau / Outre mesure, tr.: Anthony Hartley. *The Penguin Book of French Verse 4, The Twentieth Century,* introduced and edited by Anthony Hartley. Harmondsworth: Penguin Books Ltd., 1959.

The Invasion / That Memory / Clear Winter / A Lot of People / Endless Journeys / Love Again, tr.: John Ashbery. *Evergreen Review,* January–February 1960.

Crève-Cœur, from *Cale sèche* / Saltimbanques, from *Poèmes en prose* / Un Homme fini, from *La Balle au bond* / Longue Portée, from *Le Chant des morts,* tr.: Elaine Marks. *French Poetry from Baudelaire to the Present,* with English prose translations; introduced and edited by Elaine Marks; Germaine Brée, general editor, French Series. New York: The Laurel Language Library, Dell Publishing Co., 1962.

Quai aux fleurs, tr.: J. Kennedy. *Chelsea,* March 1962.

Francis Ponge

Born in 1899 at Montpellier. Spent childhood in Avignon. Continued secondary studies in Paris, where his father became professor of English in the Lycée Condorcet. Studied letters at the university. Had associations with the surrealists and the *Nouvelle Revue Française*. Employed in the publishing business and in journalism. Organized the resistance movement of journalists during World War II. Since 1952 a professor at the Alliance Française of Paris. Lecture tours in Belgium, Germany, Italy, and Yugoslavia.

MAIN WORKS

Le Parti-pris des choses. Paris: Editions Gallimard, 1942, 1949.

Dix Courts sur la méthode. Paris: Editions Pierre Seghers, 1946.

Le Carnet du bois de pins, essai poétique. Lausanne: Mermod, 1947.

Proèmes. Paris: Editions Gallimard, 1948.
Le Peintre à l'étude. Paris: Editions Gallimard, 1948.
Le Verre d'eau, recueil de notes et de lithographies. Paris: Galerie Louise Leiris, 1949.
Le Grand Recueil. Paris: Editions Gallimard, 1961.

TO CONSULT

Sartre, J.-P.: *L'Homme et les choses.* Paris: Seghers, 1947.
Schneider, P.: Introduction to the Works of Francis Ponge. *Transition Fifty,* no. 6, 1950.
Gros, L.-G.: "Francis Ponge ou le parti pris des choses," *Les Poètes contemporains.* Paris: Cahiers du Sud, 1951.
Hommage à Francis Ponge. Paris: NRF, Gallimard, 1956.
Douthat, M.: "Francis Ponge's Untenable Goat," *Yale French Studies,* no. 21, 1958.
Sollers, P.: *Francis Ponge.* Paris: Seghers, 1963.

TRANSLATIONS

A New Introduction to the Pebble, tr.: Paul Bowles. *View,* VI, no. 4, November 1945.
The Pebble / Introduction to the Pebble / A Letter to Bernard Groethuysen, *Essays on Language and Literature: M. Proust, P. Valéry, J.-P. Sartre, J. Paulhan, F. Ponge, B. Parain,* edited by J. L. Havesi. London: Allan Wingate 1947.
L'Allumette / L'Appareil du téléphone / La Grenouille / Grand Nu sous bois, tr.: Wallace Fowlie. *Poetry,* September 1952.

The Goat, from *Le Parti-pris des choses,* tr.: H. Richarson. *Yale French Studies,* no. 21, 1958.

Le Tronc d'arbre / Les Trois Boutiques / L'Huître / Le Papillon / Notes pour un coquillage, tr.: Anthony Hartley. *The Penguin Book of French Verse 4, The Twentieth Century,* introduced and edited by Anthony Hartley. Harmondsworth: Penguin Books Ltd., 1959.

Seven Poems by Francis Ponge, Snails / Rain / Berries / The Quart Box / The Orange / The Turning of the Seasons / Notes for a Shell, tr.: Richard Strawn. *New Directions in Prose and Poetry,* no. 21, 1961.

La Fin de l'automne / La Cigarette, from *Le Parti-pris des choses,* tr.: Elaine Marks. *French Poetry from Baudelaire to the Present,* with English prose translations; introduced and edited by Elaine Marks; Germaine Brée, general editor, French Series. New York: The Laurel Language Library, Dell Publishing Co., 1962.

Jacques Audiberti

Born in 1899 at Antibes on the Mediterranean. Journalist in Paris since 1925. Received the Prix Mallarmé for poetry in 1935 and the Prix de la critique in 1964. Officer of the Legion of Honor. Successful playwright, novelist, as well as poet. Lives part of the year in Paris, part in his home town on the Mediterranean.

MAIN WORKS

L'Empire et la trappe. Paris: Crès; Picard, 1929.

Race des hommes. Paris: Collection Métamorphoses, Nouvelle Revue Française, 1937.

Des Tonnes de semence. Paris: Nouvelle Revue Française, 1941.

Urujac, roman. Paris: Nouvelle Revue Française, 1941.

La Nouvelle Origine. Paris: Nouvelle Revue Française, 1942.

Toujours. Paris: Editions Gallimard, 1943.

La Pluie sur les boulevards. Angers: Au Masque d'Or, 1950.

Rempart. Paris: Collection Blanche, Editions Gallimard, 1953.

La Beauté de l'amour, roman en vers. Paris: Editions Gallimard, 1955.

Les Tombeaux ferment mal, roman. Paris: Editions Gallimard, 1964.

Ange aux entrailles, poésies. Paris: Editions Gallimard, 1964.

TO CONSULT

"Jacques Audiberti," *Biblio.* Paris: Librairie Hachette, mars 1963.

Cornell, K.: "Audiberti and Obscurity," *Yale French Studies,* no. 4, 1949.

Wellwarth, G.: "Jacques Audiberti; The Drama of the Savage God," *Texas Studies in Literature and Language,* IV, no. 3, Autumn 1962.

Deslandes, A.: *Audiberti.* Paris: La Bibliothèque Idéale, Gallimard, 1964.

Selective Bibliography

Henri Michaux

Born in 1899 at Namur, Belgium, in a middle-class family. Studied at Brussels. Abandoning medical studies, went traveling as a sailor. Visited North and South American ports, returned to Brussels and started writing. In 1924 settled in Paris, continued traveling, discovered surrealist painters as well as Asia, and was hailed by André Gide. Married in 1942, death of his wife in 1948. Has been drawing and painting regularly since 1937 and experimenting with hallucinatory drugs since 1956.

MAIN WORKS

Un Barbare en Asie. Paris: Editions Gallimard, 1933.

La Nuit remue. Paris: Editions Gallimard, 1935.

Voyage en grande Garabagne. Paris: Editions Gallimard, 1936.

Plume, précédé de *Lointain Intérieur*. Paris: Editions Gallimard, 1938, 1948.

Labyrinthes. Paris: R. J. Godet, 1943, 1944.

Espace du dedans, extraits (*Qui je fus, Ecuador, La Nuit remue, Plume, Voyage en grande Garabagne, Au Pays de la magie, Peintures*). Paris: Editions Gallimard, 1944.

Epreuves, exorcismes. Paris: Editions Gallimard, 1945.

La Vie dans les plis. Paris: Editions Gallimard, 1949.

Passages. Paris: Editions Gallimard, 1950, 1964.

Nouvelles de l'étranger. Paris: Mercure de France, 1952.

Face aux verrous. Paris: Editions Gallimard, 1954.

L'infini turbulent. Paris: Mercure de France, 1957.

Paix dans les brisements, 14 dessins suivis d'un texte explicatif et d'un poème. Paris: Flinker, 1959.

Connaissance par les gouffres. Paris: Editions Gallimard, 1961.

Vents et poussières, 1955–1962. Paris: Flinker, 1962.

TO CONSULT

Gide, A.: *Découvrons Henri Michaux.* Paris: Gallimard, 1941.

Bertelé, R.: *Henri Michaux.* Paris: Pierre Seghers, 1946.

Ellmann, R.: "The Ductile Universe of Henri Michaux," *Kenyon Review,* 1948.

Coulon, P.: *Henri Michaux, poète de notre société.* Neuchâtel: La Baconnière, 1949.

Hoog, A.: "Henri Michaux, or Mythic Symbolism," *Yale French Studies,* no. 9, 1952.

Bréchon, R.: *Henri Michaux,* Bibliothèque Idéale, NRF. Paris: Gallimard, 1959.

Mills, R.: "Char and Michaux: Magicians of Insecurity," *Chicago Review,* xv, 1961.

Harvey, L.: "Michaux's 'Chant de Mort,'" *Explicator,* xx, 1, 1961.

Hackett, C. A.: "Michaux and Plume," *Yale French Studies,* no. 17, January 1963.

Bishop, L.: "Michaux's 'Clown,'" *French Review,* no. 3, December 1963.

TRANSLATIONS

Plume's Vision, tr.: Stewart Gilbert. *Transition,* no. 21, March 1932.

There is, tr.: Lionel Abel / The Book of Strange Situations (from *Pays de la Magie*), tr.: Felix Giovanelli. *View*, VI, nos. 2–3, March–April 1946.

And More Changes Still, tr.: Richard Ellmann. *Partisan Review*, Spring 1946.

Revelations, tr.: Richard Ellmann. *Partisan Review*, December 1946.

The Peaceful Man / Plume at the Restaurant / Plume Takes a Trip / The Night of the Bulgarians, tr.: Lloyd Alexander. *New Directions*, no. 10, 1948.

Cries / The Enanglom / The Heroic Age / The Night of the Bulgarians / Plume Travels / Simplicity / MNA / Bridal Night / In the Land of the Hais, tr.: Richard Ellmann. *Sewanee Review*, 1948.

Projection / Nausea / Or Is It Death Coming? / The Nonays and the Oliabarians / Magic, tr.: Richard Ellmann. *Yale French Studies*, no. 2, 1948.

The Jetty, tr.: Richard Ellmann. *Poetry*, February 1949.

I am writing to you from a distant land, tr.: Richard Ellmann. *Sewanee Review*, 1949.

A Barbarian in Asia (*Un Barbare en Asie*), tr.: Sylvia Beach. New York: New Directions, 1949.

The Hivinizikis, from *Voyage to Great Garaban*, tr.: Richard Ellmann. *Hudson Review*, Winter 1949.

In the Land of Magic, tr.: Richard Ellmann. *Kenyon Review*, 1949.

The March into the Tunnel, tr.: Richard Ellmann. *Partisan Review*, July 1949.

My Properties, tr.: Richard Ellmann. *Hudson Review*, Spring 1949.

Impulses, tr.: E. Clark. *100 Modern Poems,* Selden Rodman, comp. Chicago: Pellegrini and Cudahy, 1949.

The Motorcycles, tr.: not given. *Neurotica* (N.Y.), no. 7, 1949.

Selected Writings: The Space Within, tr.: Richard Ellmann. New York: New Directions, 1950.

In the Land of Magic, tr.: Richard Ellmann. *Little Treasury of World Poetry,* Hubert Creekmore, editor. New York: Charles Scribner's Sons, 1952.

A Very Small Horse, tr.: Richard Ellmann. *New Directions in Prose and Poetry,* 1953.

Ulp and Alp / The Lock-eating Animal / The Executioner / Nature Faithful to Man / Vision / Ecce Homo, tr.: Richard Ellmann. *Wake,* VI, 1953.

My Occupation (Mes Occupations) / Death Chant (Chant de mort) / Fate (Destinée) / A Peaceful Man (Un Homme paisible) / Plume Traveling (Plume voyage) / I am writing you from a distant land (Je vous écris d'un pays lointain) / Clown, tr.: Wallace Fowlie. *Mid-Century French Poets.* New York: Grove Press, 1955.

From "Misérable Miracle," tr.: Louise Varèse. *Paris Review,* Winter 1957.

Nausée ou c'est la mort qui vient? / La Jeune Fille de Budapest / La Lettre / Labyrinthe / Voix, tr.: Anthony Hartley. *The Penguin Book of French Verse 4, The Twentieth Century,* introduced and edited by Anthony Hartley. Harmondsworth: Penguin Books Ltd., 1959.

Experiment 5, tr.: Paul Gregory. *New World Writing,* June 1959.

Contre, tr.: Cecily Mackworth. *Times Literary Supplement,* October 13, 1961.

Mon Roi, from *La Nuit remue* / Dans la nuit / Un Homme paisible, from *Plume* / Immense Voix, from *Exercices, exorcismes,* tr.: Elaine Marks. *French Poetry from Baudelaire to the Present,* with English prose translations, introduced and edited by Elaine Marks; Germaine Brée, general editor, French Series. New York: The Laurel Language Library, Dell Publishing Co., 1962.

Four Poems, Poetry for Power: I row / Across Deserts and Seas / Lazarus, Are You Asleep / In the Night, tr.: Louise Varèse. *Chicago Review,* Autumn 1962.

The Thin Man, from *Vigies sur cibles,* tr., Charles Guenther. *Chelsea,* Special French Issue, June 1963.

Misérable miracle; mescaline, with eight drawings by the author, tr.: Louise Varèse. San Francisco: City Light Books, 1963.

Two Poems from Ecuador, tr.: R. Magowan. *Poetry Northwest,* Winter 1964.

Jean Follain

Born in 1903 at Canisy, Normandy, in a family of provincial notaries and school teachers. Secondary studies in the Collège of Saint-Lô. Settled in Paris in 1925, continuing law studies begun at Caen. Was admitted to the bar in 1928 and joined a group of young writers associated with the review *Sagesse.* Had marginal contacts with surrealists, closer ties with André Salmon, Max Jacob, Géo Charles. Became district judge in the forties. Retired, lives in Paris.

MAIN WORKS

Paris. Paris: Editions Corréa, 1935.
Chants terrestres. Paris: Editions Denoël, 1937.
L'Épicerie d'enfance. Paris: Editions Corréa, 1938.
Ici-bas. Bruxelles: Journal des Poètes, série poétique, 88, 1941.
Canisy. Paris: Editions Gallimard, 1942.
Inventaire. Paris: Editions Debresse, 1942.
Usage du temps. Paris: Nouvelle Revue Française, 1943.
Exister. Paris: Editions Gallimard, 1947.
Chef-Lieu. Paris: Editions Gallimard, 1950.
Les Choses données. Paris: Editions Pierre Seghers, 1952.
Territoires. Paris: Editions Gallimard, 1953.
Palais souterrain. Alès: Pab, 1953.
Objets. Limoges: Rougerie, 1955.
Tout Instant, poèmes en prose. Paris: Editions Gallimard, 1957.
Des Heures. Paris: Editions Gallimard, 1960.
Poèmes et prose choisis. Paris: Editions Gallimard, 1961.
Appareil de la terre. Paris: Editions Gallimard, 1964.

TO CONSULT

Goffin, R.: *Entrer en poésie.* Gand: Chat qui pêche, 1943.
Chapelan, M.: "Jean Follain ou les succulences de la prose," *Nouvelle Revue Française,* août 1947.
DHôtel, A.: *Jean Follain.* Paris: Seghers, 1956.

TRANSLATIONS

Self-mutilation / The Bird Stuffer / Timeless / The Fox / The Children, tr.: C. Mills and E. Sellin. *Literary Review,* Spring 1961.

Signs, tr.: W. S. Merwin. *Times Literary Supplement,* October 13, 1961.

The Girl Against the Wall, tr.: G. W. Ireland. *Times Literary Supplement,* May 4, 1962.

The Man Who Stuffed Birds, from *Exister* / Life and Death, from *Territoires* / The Sheds in the Plain / The Road / The Calm / Compass / A Shape of Time and Always, from *Cahiers du Sud,* 1962, tr.: Bernard Keith. *Chelsea,* Special French Issue, June 1963.

René Char

Born in 1907 at l'Isle-sur-Sorgue in the Vaucluse. Participated in the surrealist movement. Was resistance leader during World War II. Friend of Albert Camus; lives alternately in Paris and at l'Isle-sur-Sorgue. Has written on the art of Joan Miró, Georges Braque.

MAIN WORKS

Le Marteau sans maître. Paris: J. Corti, 1934, 1945.

Dehors la nuit est gouvernée. Paris: G.L.M., 1938, 1949.

Seuls demeurent. Paris: Editions Gallimard, 1945.

Feuillets d'Hypnos. Paris: Editions Gallimard, 1946.

Le Poème pulvérisé. Paris: Le Prat, 1947.

Fureur et mystère. Paris: Editions Gallimard, 1948.

Les Matinaux. Paris: Editions Gallimard, 1950.

A une sérénité crispée. Paris: Editions Gallimard, 1951.

La Paroi et la prairie. Paris: G.L.M., 1952.

Lettera amorosa. Paris: Collection Espoir, Editions Gallimard, 1953.

Recherche de la base et du sommet. Paris: Editions Gallimard, 1955.

Poèmes et prose choisis, 1935–1957. Paris: Editions Gallimard, 1957.

L'Inclémence lointaine. Paris: P. Berès, 1961.

La Parole en archipel, poèmes. Paris: Editions Gallimard, 1962.

Commune Présence, choix de poèmes. Paris: Editions Gallimard, 1964.

TO CONSULT

Mounin, G.: *Avez-vous lu Char?* Paris: Gallimard, 1946.

Douglas, K.: "René Char," *Yale French Studies,* no. 2, 1949.

Ménard, R.: *Interpretative Essays on Two Poems by René Char,* To a tensed serenity, Lettera amorosa, tr. Robert Fitzgerald. Rome: Editions Botteghe Oscure, n.d.

Blanchot, M., Bounoure, G., Camus, A., Mounin, G., Picon, G., Ménard, R.; *René Char's Poetry: Studies,* tr. David Paul and Robert Fitzgerald. Rome: Editions de Luca, 1956.

Rau, G.: *René Char ou la poésie accrue,* essai. Paris: J. Corti, 1957.

Fowlie, W.: "René Char and the Poet's Vocation," *Yale French Studies,* no. 21, 1958.

Bly, R.: "Some Thoughts on Lorca and Char," *The Fifties,* no. 3, 1959.

Guerre, P.: *René Char.* Paris: Seghers, 1961.
"René Char," special no. of *L'Arc,* no. 23, 1963.

TRANSLATIONS

Artine, from *Artine,* Turning, from *La Marteau sans maître,* tr.: not given. *New Directions,* no. 2, 1940.

Louis Curel de la Sorgue, tr.: Barbara Gibbs. *Partisan Review,* Spring 1946.

Farewell to the Wind, tr.: Felix Giovanelli. *View,* VI, March–April, 1946.

The Pulverized Poem, tr.: not given. *Transition Forty-Eight,* no. 1, January 1948.

Medallion / So That Nothing May Be Changed / Youth / Anniversary / Duty / Gravity, tr.: Lloyd Alexander. *New Directions in Prose and Poetry,* 1948.

Wind Away (Congé au vent) / The Basket-Weaver's Love (La Compagne du Vannier) / Youth (Jeunesse) / Living (Conduite) / Postscript (Post scriptum) / Hymn in a Low Voice (Hymne à voix basse) / Lily of the Valley (Le Muguet) / Martha (Marthe) / To the Health of the Serpent (A la santé du serpent) / The Meteor of the 13th of August (Le Météore du 13 août) / To an Image of Warrior Ardour (A une ferveur belliqueuse) / Flushed with joy, those that rise in the Morning . . . (Rougeur des matinaux) / Divergence (Divergence) / The Advice of the Lookout (Conseil de la sentinelle) / Pyrenees (Pyrénées) / On Leave (Le Permissionnaire) / Nights of Fulfillment (Les Nuits justes) / Wherefore yield? (Pourquoi se rendre?), tr.: Denis

Devlin and Jackson Mathews. *Botteghe Oscure,* x, 1952.

Anniversary / Violences, tr.: Felix Giovanelli. *New Directions in Prose and Poetry,* 1953.

L'Absent / Par la bouche de l'engoulevent / Ne s'entend pas / Louis Curel de la Sorgue / Force clémente / Le Devoir / Le Loriot / Eléments / La Liberté, from *Seuls demeurent,* trs.: Emile Snyder and Donald Young. *Western Review,* Autumn 1953.

Leaves of Hypnos (*Feuillets d'Hypnos*), extracts: A War Journal (1943–1944), Lettera amorosa, tr.: Jackson Mathews. *Botteghe Oscure,* no. XIV, 1954.

The Damaged Crop / If a Forest / The Prodigal's Torch / Fine Edifice and Forebodings / Sturdy Meteors / The Oriole / A March / Threshold / Song of the Corduroy / The Revelation / Fascinating Four, tr.: Charles Guenther. *Quarterly Review of Literature,* 8, no. 3, 1955.

Hypnos Waking, poetry and prose, selected and tr. by Jackson Mathews, with the collaboration of William Carlos Williams, Richard Wilbur, William Jay Smith, Barbara Howes, W. S. Merwin, and James Wright. New York: Random House, 1956. Contents: Congé au vent / La Compagne du vannier / Jeunesse / Le Loriot / Fenaison / Les Transparents, tr.: Richard Wilbur; L'Alouette / Complainte du lézard amoureux / Jouvence des Névons / Sur les hauteurs / Dédale / La Vérité vous rendra libres, tr.: Barbara Howes; L'Amoureuse en secret / Les Seigneurs de Maussane / Toute Vie, tr.: James Wright; Pyrénées / Le Permissionnaire / Les Nuits justes / Pleinement / Le Tout ensemble / Hermétiques Ouvriers / Montagne déchirée / Fête des arbres et du chasseur, tr.: William J. Smith; Mission et révocation, I–LV, from *Partage formel* // Conduite / Gravité / Le Visage nuptial / Evadne / Post-Scriptum, from *Le Visage nuptial* // La Rose de chêne, from *Feuillets d'Hypnos* // Argument / Les Trois sœurs / Biens égaux / Donnerbach Muhle / Hymne à voix basse / J'habite une douleur / Le Muguet / Seuil / L'Extravagant / Pulvérin / Affres détonation silence / Le Bulletin des Baux / Le Requin et la mouette / Marthe / Suzerain / A la santé du serpent / L'Age de roseau / Chanson du velours à côtes / Le Météore du 13 août / Lyre / Arrière-histoire du poème pulvérisé, from *Le Poème pulvérisé* // Dédicace / Sur le franc-bord, from *Lettera amorosa,* tr.: Jackson Mathews; Madeleine qui veillait, tr.: William Carlos Williams; Vers l'arbre-frère aux jours comptés, tr.: William Carlos Williams; Le Rempart de brindilles / L'Inoffensif / Le Mortel Partenaire / La Double Tresse / Sur le Tympan d'une église romane / Le Vipereau / Victoire éclair / Vermillon / La Chambre dans l'espace / Le Deuil des Névons / Pourquoi la journée vole, tr.: W. S. Merwin.

The Inventors / The Windowpane / Put on Guard / Anoupis and Later Jeanne / The Slapped Adolescent / Coral, from *Les Matinaux,* tr.: Charles Guenther. *Poetry,* March 1957.

The Man Who Walked in a Ray of Sunshine, tr.: Roger Shattuck. *Botteghe Oscure,* xix, 1957.

Lascaux: Homme-oiseau et bison mourant / Les Cerfs noirs, La Bête innommable, Jeune Cheval à la crinière vaporeuse / Transir / Quatre Fascinants: Le Taureau, La Truite, Le Serpent, L'Alouette / La Minutieuse, from *La Paroi et la prairie,* tr.: David Paul. *Hudson Review,* Spring 1958.

On a Night without Adornment, tr.: Charles Guenther. *Quarterly Review of Literature,* 9, no. 3, 1958.

To a Tensed Serenity (A une sérénité crispée), tr.: Bradford Cook. *Botteghe Oscure,* XXII, 1958.

Companions in the Garden (To André du Bouchet et Jacques Dupin), tr.: Charles Guenther. *Poetry,* April 1959.

Les Inventeurs / Pyrénées / Seuil / Redonnez-leur / La Sorgue, tr.: Anthony Hartley. *The Penguin Book of French Verse 4, The Twentieth Century,* introduced and edited by Anthony Hartley. Harmondsworth: Penguin Books Ltd., 1959.

Sur les hauteurs, from *Fureur et mystère* // Lascaux: Homme-oiseau mort et bison mourant, Les Cerfs noirs, La Bête innommable, Jeune Cheval à la crinière vaporeuse, from *La Paroi et la prairie* // Divergence / La Vérité vous rendra libres, from *Fureur et mystère,* tr.: Robert Bly. *The Sixties,* no. 5, 1961.

Congé au vent, from *Seuls demeurent* // Marthe, from *Le Poème pulvérisé* // Si les pommes de terre ne se reproduisent plus, from *A une sérénité crispée,* tr.: Elaine Marks. *French Poetry from Baudelaire to the Present,* with English prose translations, introduced and edited by Elaine Marks; Germaine Brée, gen-

eral editor, French Series. New York: The Laurel Language Library, Dell Publishing Co., 1962.
The Schoolgirl, tr.: Charles Guenther. *Minnesota Review,* Autumn 1962.
The Library Is on Fire, from *Poèmes et prose choisis,* tr.: Charles Guenther. *Chelsea,* Special French Issue, June 1963.
Chanson des étages / Post-Scriptum à Lettera amorosa / Sept Parcelles de Luberon / Les Parages d'Alsace, tr.: Wallace Fowlie. *Poetry,* August 1964.

André Frénaud

Born in 1907 at Montceau-les-Mines. Studied philosophy and law. Lecturer on French at the University of Lwów in Poland in 1930. Numerous journeys in Europe. A German prisoner in 1940, worked in a war camp in Brandenburg. In 1942 escaped to France and participated in the Resistance. Active as a public official.

MAIN WORKS

Les Rois mages. Paris: Editions Pierre Seghers, 1943.
Soleil irréductible. Neuchâtel-Paris: Ides et Calendes, 1946.
La Noce noire. Paris: Editions Pierre Seghers, 1947.
La Femme de ma vie. Paris: A. Blaizot, 1947.
Poèmes de dessous le plancher. Paris: Editions Gallimard, 1949.
Les Paysans. Paris: Jean Aubier, 1951.
Source entière. Paris: Editions Pierre Seghers, 1953.
Passage de la visitation. Paris: Levis Mano, 1956.
Agonie du Général Krivitski. Paris: P. J. Oswald, 1960.

Pour l'office des morts. Alès: Pab, 1961.

Il n'y a pas de paradis, poèmes. Paris: Editions Gallimard, 1962.

TO CONSULT

Gros, L.-G.: "André Frénaud," *Cahiers du Sud,* no. 28, 1944.

Lescure, J.: "A. Frénaud ou la poésie à hauteur d'homme," *Poésie,* nos. 22–23, 1945.

Clancier, G.-E.: *André Frénaud.* Paris: Seghers, 1953.

TRANSLATIONS

Da-Sein / Hatefully My Love Poetry, tr.: Barbara Gibbs. *Partisan Review,* Spring 1946.

Night (Veille), tr.: Wallace Fowlie. *Poetry,* September 1952.

Fraternité / Exhortation aux pauvres / Je ne t'ai jamais oubliée, tr.: Anthony Hartley. *The Penguin Book of French Verse 4, The Twentieth Century,* introduced and edited by Anthony Hartley. Harmondsworth: Penguin Books Ltd., 1959.

Eugène Guillevic

Born in 1907 at Carnac, Brittany. Secondary studies in Altkirch, Alsace, near Ferrette. Began career as civil servant at twenty, was promoted in 1935 to post in Central Administration of Finances in Paris. Discovered poetry through Baudelaire, Claudel, Eluard. Turned to atheism after religious crisis in 1932; friendship with Marcel Arland, Drieu la Rochelle, and Eluard.

Selective Bibliography

MAIN WORKS

Requiem. Paris: Tschamm, 1938.
Terraqué. Paris: Editions Gallimard, 1942.
Amulettes. Paris: Editions Pierre Seghers, 1946.
Exécutoire. Paris: Editions Gallimard, 1947.
Fractures. Paris: Editions de Minuit, 1947.
Les Chansons d'Antonin Blond. Paris: Editions Pierre Seghers, 1949.
Envie de vivre. Paris: Editions Pierre Seghers, 1951.
Terre à bonheur. Paris: Editions Pierre Seghers, 1953.
31 sonnets. Paris: Editions Gallimard, 1954.
Carnac. Paris: Editions Gallimard, 1961.

TO CONSULT

Gros, L.-G.: *Poètes contemporains.* Paris: Cahiers du Sud, 1951.
Daix, P.: *Guillevic.* Paris: Poètes d'aujourd'hui, Seghers, 1954.

TRANSLATIONS

Lidice / Object Lesson / Season / We're Hopeful / Banners, tr.: Kenneth O. Hanson. *California Quarterly,* Winter 1953.
Monsters, from *Monstres. Times Literary Supplement,* February 11, 1955.
Face / News Item / Life Grows / Awareness / Amulets, tr.: Emile Snyder. *Literary Review,* Spring 1961.
There Are Monsters / Quartered Beef, tr.: Emile Snyder. *Chelsea,* Special French Issue, June 1963.

André Pieyre de Mandiargues

Born in 1909 in Paris. Grandson of Paul Bernard, collector of impressionist paintings. Dropped out of school to study archeology. Lived alone before World War II, traveled throughout Europe and the Mediterranean Orient. After the armistice moved to Monte Carlo. Returned to Paris after the war, married, joined the surrealist group headed by André Breton and continued to work intensely and to travel. Well known also as a novelist.

MAIN WORKS

Dans les années sordides. Monaco, 1943; Paris: Editions Gallimard, 1949.

Le Musée noir. Paris: Editions Pauvert, 1947, 1957.

Soleil des loups. Paris: Editions Pauvert, 1946, 1951, Editions Laffont, 1957.

Les Incongruités monumentales. Paris: Editions Laffont, 1948.

Marbre, Paris: Editions Laffont, 1953.

Le Lis de mer, récit. Paris: Editions Laffont, 1956, 1962.

Astyanax. Paris: Editions du Terrain Vague, 1957, Editions Gallimard 1964.

Les Monstres de Bomarso. Paris: Editions Grasset, 1957.

Le Cadran lunaire. Paris: Editions Laffont, 1958.

Le Belvédère. Paris: Editions Grasset, 1958.

Feu de braise, contes. Paris: Editions Grasset, 1959.

Sugai. Paris: Le Musée de poche, G. Fall, 1960.

L'Age de craie, suivi de *Hedera.* Paris: Editions Gallimard, 1961.

Deuxième Belvédère. Paris: Editions Grasset, 1962.

La Motocyclette, roman. Paris: Editions Gallimard, 1963.

TO CONSULT

Arland, M.: *Nouvelles lettres de France.* Paris: Albin Michel, 1954.

Selz, J.: "Pieyre de Mandiargues et l'esthétique de la représentation," *Lettres nouvelles,* janvier 1958.

Berger, Y.: "Le Théâtre d'André Pieyre de Mandiargues," *Nouvelle Revue Française,* novembre 1959.

Gascht, A.: *André Pieyre de Mandiargues, ou le Goût de l'insolite.* Bruxelles: Marginale, 1961.

Tremmer, M. J.: "André Pieyre de Mandiargues," *Yale French Studies,* no. 31, 1964.

TRANSLATIONS

The Passageway of Judiciary Pleasures, from *Dans les années sordides,* tr.: Paul Bowles. *View,* VI, March–April 1946.

The Girl Beneath the Lion (*Le Lis de mer*), novel, tr.: Richard Howard. New York: Grove Press, 1958.

Childishness, tr.: Richard Howard. *Evergreen Review,* Autumn 1958.

The Diamond, tr.: Richard Howard. *Evergreen Review,* January–February 1962.

René Guy Cadou

Born in 1920 at Sainte-Reine in Brittany, son of a school teacher. From 1930 to 1938 received secondary education in Nantes. Failed at baccalauréat examinations. Became elementary school teacher, living and teaching in several places near Nantes. Was associated with a group of young poets and critics who used to meet in 1943 at Rochefort-sur-Loire (Ecole de Rochefort). Met Hélène in 1943. Took directions from the poetry of Apollinaire, Francis Jammes, Max Jacob and Pierre Reverdy. Visited Paris only once, in 1946. Published numerous articles in literary journals. Died in 1951 at Louisfert near Nantes.

MAIN WORKS

Grand Elan. Niort: Nicolas, 1943.
La Vie rêvée. Paris: Editions Laffont, 1944.
Pleine Poitrine. Périgueux: Faulac, 1946.
Poèmes choisis, 1944–1950. Nantes: Chiffoleau, 1950.
Les Biens de ce monde, 1944–1950. Paris: Editions Pierre Seghers, 1951.
Usage interne. Paris: Aux amis de Rochefort, Debresse, 1952.
Hélène ou le règne végétal. Paris: Editions Pierre Seghers, 1952.
La Maison d'été. Paris: Nouv. Edit. Debresse, 1955.
Florilège poétique, établi et présenté par Georges Bouquet et Pierre Ménanteau. Paris: Editions Pierre Seghers, 1957.
Le Cœur définitif. Paris: Editions Pierre Seghers, 1961.
Poésie la vie entière, tome I: 1937–1942. Fay-aux-Loges, Loiret: coll. Les Amis de Rochefort, Cahiers de Rochefort, Bonhier, 1961.

TO CONSULT

Clancier, G. A.: "Le nom de Cadou," *Art*, April 24, 1953.

Manoll, M.: *René Guy Cadou.* Paris: Seghers, 1954.
René Guy Cadou, témoignages et souvenirs. Paris: L'Herne, 1961.

TRANSLATIONS

I will take you across my saddle, tr.: Kenneth Rexroth. *New Directions in Prose and Poetry,* 1955.
Poème d'amour à Hélène / Source de vie / Celui qui entre par hasard, tr.: Anthony Hartley, *The Penguin Book of French Verse 4, The Twentieth Century,* introduced and edited by Anthony Hartley. Harmondsworth: Penguin Books Ltd., 1959.
December Evening / The Events of the Play / Is It Christ or a Friend? / Landscape of My Love / O My Father I Had Chosen, tr.: Charles Guenther. *Literary Review,* Spring 1961.
The Dogs That Dream / Poetic Art / Speechless / Helen or the Vegetable Kingdom / Faces of the Earth, from *Hélène ou le règne végétal,* tr.: Charles Guenther. *Chelsea,* Special French Issue, June 1963.

Yves Bonnefoy

Born in 1923. Secondary studies at Tours, mathematics at the University of Poitiers, philosophy at the University of Paris. From 1945–47 frequented the surrealists, read Chestov and Kierkegaard, discovered the Tuscan primitives. Travels: Italy, England, Spain, Greece, United States. Art history studies: French mural painting of the Middle Ages, Italian art. Translated Shakespeare. A leading French critic of poetry and a visiting professor at Brandeis University from 1962 to 1964. Lives in Paris.

MAIN WORKS

Traité du pianiste. Paris: La Révolution la nuit, 1946.
Du Mouvement et de l'immobilité de Douve. Paris: Mercure de France, 1953.
Peintures murales de la France gothique. Paris: P. Hartmann, 1954.
W. Shakespeare: *Henri IV, Jules César,* traductions. Paris: Club Français du Livre, 1957.
W. Shakespeare: *Hamlet,* traduction. Paris: Club Français du Livre, 1958.
Hier régnant désert. Paris: Mercure de France, 1958.
Pierre écrite. Paris: Maeght, 1959.
L'Improbable, essais. Paris: Mercure de France, 1959.
La Seconde Simplicité, essais. Paris: Mercure de France, 1961.
Rimbaud par lui-même, coll. Ecrivains de toujours. Paris: Editions du Seuil, 1961.
Pierre écrite. Paris: Mercure de France, 1964.

TO CONSULT

Saillet, M.: "Du Mouvement et de l'immobilité de Douve," *Lettres nouvelles,* novembre 1953.
Duits, Ch.: "L'Enigme poétique d'Yves Bonnefoy," *Critique,* no. 137, 1958.
Maurin, M.: "On Bonnefoy's Poetry," *Yale French Studies,* no. 21, 1958.
Richard, J.-P.: "Yves Bonnefoy entre le nombre et la nuit," *Critique,* mai 1961.

Brée, G.: "New French Poetry," *New French Writing.* New York: Criterion Books, 1961.

TRANSLATIONS

Cinq Poèmes, tr.: Wallace Fowlie. *Poetry,* September 1952.

Vrai Nom (Real Name), tr.: Simon Watson Taylor. *The Atlantic Monthly,* June 1958.

Aux Arbres / Douve parle / Hic est locus patriae / Lieu de combat, tr.: Anthony Hartley. *The Penguin Book of French Verse, 4, The Twentieth Century,* introduced and edited by Anthony Hartley. Harmondsworth: Penguin Books, Ltd., 1959.

Théâtre I–XIX / Aux Arbres / Le Seul Témoin / Vrai Nom / Phénix / Vrai Corps / Art poétique, from *Derniers Gestes* / Selections from *Du Mouvement et de l'immobilité de Douve,* tr.: Galway Kinnell. *Hudson Review,* Winter 1960–61.

Lieu de la Salamandre, from *Du Mouvement et de l'immobilité de Douve,* tr.: Galway Kinnell. *The Sixties,* no. 5, 1961.

Quelle parole a surgi près de moi (What word sprang up beside me) / Une Voix (A Voice) / Une Autre Voix (Another Voice) / Si cette nuit est autre que la nuit (If this night is other than the night) / Douve Parle (Douve Speaks) / Demande au maître de la nuit quelle est cette nuit (Ask the master of the night what is this night) / Voix basses et Phénix (Low Voices and Phoenix) / Mais que se taise celle qui veille encore (But let her be silent, the one still watching) / Tais-toi puisqu'aussi bien nous sommes de la nuit (Be still, for surely we are the most) / from Douve parle, in *Du Mouvement et de l'immobilité de Douve;* Ainsi marcherons-nous sur les ruines d'un ciel immense (Thus we will walk on the ruins of a vast sky) / La Salamandre (The Salamander) / Quand reparut la salamandre, le soleil (When the salamander reappeared, the sun) / Cassandre, dira-t-il, mains désertes et peintes (Cassandra, he will say, hands empty and painted) / Justice / Je prendrai dans mes mains ta face morte (I will take your dead face in my hands) / L'orangerie sera ta résidence (The orangery shall be your dwelling-place) / Vérité (Truth) / Tu as pris une lampe et tu ouvres la porte (You took a lamp and you open the door), from L'Orangerie in *Du Mouvement et de l'immobilité de Douve;* Qu'une place soit faite à celui qui approche (Let a place be made ready for the one who approaches) / Lieu du Combat (Place of Battle) / Lieu de la salamandre (Place of the Salamander) / Vrai Lieu du cerf (True Place of the Stag) / Le jour franchit le soir, il gagnera (Day breaks over evening, it shall sweep beyond), from Vrai Lieu in *Du Mouvement et de l'immobilité de Douve,* tr. Galway Kinnell. *Poetry,* July 1962.

A San Francesco, le soir (San Francesco, at Night) from Menaces du témoin in *Hier régnant désert;* Le jour se penche sur le fleuve du passé (Day bends over the river of the past) / Il y a que la lampe brûlait bas (There's this: the lamp was burning low) / Le

Pont de fer (The Iron Bridge) from Le Visage mortel in *Hier régnant désert;* Ici, toujours ici (Here, still here) from A une terre d'aube in *Hier régnant désert,* tr.: Jackson Mathews. *Poetry,* July 1962.

Art poétique / Le Jour franchit le soir, il gagnera, from *Du Mouvement et de l'immobilité de Douve* / La Beauté / Toute la nuit, from *Hier régnant désert,* tr.: Elaine Marks. *French Poetry from Baudelaire to the Present,* with English prose translations, introduced and edited by Elaine Marks; Germaine Brée, general editor, French Series. New York: The Laurel Language Library, Dell Publishing Co., 1962.

True Name, tr.: Edward Lucie-Smith. *The Listener,* February 1962.

The Leave Illuminated, tr.: Edward Lucie-Smith. *Critical Quarterly,* Autumn 1963.

André du Bouchet

Born in 1924 in Paris. Studied in Paris and at the Collège of Dreux. Lived in the United States 1941–1948. A Harvard graduate of 1943. In Paris since 1948. Has published articles in literary criticism and translated Hölderlin, Shakespeare, and James Joyce into French.

MAIN WORKS

Le Moteur blanc. Paris: G.L.M., 1946, 1956.

Au Deuxième Etage. Paris: Le Dragon, 1946.

Sans couvercle. Paris: G.L.M., 1953.

Cette Surface. Alès: Impr. Benoit, 1956.

Sol de la montagne. Paris: Jean Hughes, 1956.

Dans la chaleur vacante. Paris: Mercure de France, 1959, 1961.

Sur le pas. Paris: Iliazd, 1960.

Poèmes de Hölderlin, traductions. Paris: Mercure de France, 1963.

TO CONSULT

Jaccottet, Ph.: "La poésie d'André du Bouchet," *Nouvelle Revue Française,* novembre 1957.

Bonnefoy, Y.: "La poésie d'André du Bouchet," *Critique,* avril 1962.

Richard, J.-P.: "André du Bouchet et la démesure humaine," *Mercure de France,* mai 1962.

TRANSLATIONS

Poems, tr.: not given, *Transition Fifty,* no. 6, 1950.

The Room / The Wing the Wind / Fire, from *Two Cities,* Spring 1960, tr.: Serge Gavronsky. *Chelsea,* Special French Issue, June 1963.

Philippe Jaccottet

Born in 1925 at Moudon, Switzerland. Studied liberal arts at the University of Lausanne. Went to Paris in 1946 as collaborator of Mermod editions. Traveled in Spain and Italy. Since his marriage in 1953 lives in Grignan in Drôme (France). Translator of Musil and Homer, and a critic for the Lausanne *Gazette* and the N.R.F.

MAIN WORKS

Requiem. Lausanne: Mermod, Paris, Dépôt, Julliard, Sequana, 1947.

Selective Bibliography

L'Effraie et autres poésies. Paris: Editions Gallimard, 1953.

La Promenade sous les arbres. Lausanne: Mermod, 1957.

L'Ignorant, poèmes 1952–1956. Paris: Editions Gallimard, 1957.

Eléments d'un songe. Paris: Editions Gallimard, 1961.

L'Obscurité, récit. Paris: Editions Gallimard, 1961.

La Semaison, carnets 1954–62. Lausanne: Payot, 1963.

TO CONSULT

Leyris, P.: "Un Serviteur du visible," *Cahiers des Saisons,* no. 13.

Masui, J.: "L'Espérance poétique de Philippe Jaccottet," *Cahiers du Sud,* no. 344, 1957.

Gros, L.-G.: "Philippe Jaccottet et la métaphysique quotidienne," *Cahiers du Sud,* no. 346, 1957.

TRANSLATIONS

Comme je suis un étranger dans notre vie, from *L'Effraie et autres poésies,* tr.: Elaine Marks. *French Poetry from Baudelaire to the Present,* with English prose translations, introduced and edited by Elaine Marks; Germaine Brée, general editor, French Series. New York: The Laurel Language Library, Dell Publishing Co., 1962.

Jacques Dupin

Born in 1927 at Privas, Ardèche, southern France. Settled in Paris in 1945. After studying law and political science, began to write poetry and art criticism. Was editorial secretary of the review *Empédocle* and *Cahiers d'Art.* Is editorial director of the Galerie Maeght publications in Paris. Friend of Georges Braque and René Char. Author of studies on Miró and Giacometti.

MAIN WORKS

Cendrier du voyage. Paris, G.L.M., 1951.
Art poétique. Alès: Impr. Benoit, 1956.
Les Brisants. Paris: Lévis Mano, 1958.
L'Epervier. Paris: G.L.M., 1960.
Gravir. Paris: Editions Gallimard, 1963.

TO CONSULT

J.-P. Richard: "La poésie de Jacques Dupin," *Mercure de France,* octobre 1963.

TRANSLATIONS

Joan Miró, Life and Work, tr.: Norbert Guterman. New York: Harry N. Abrams, 1962.
Alberto Giacometti, Bilingual Edition, English tr.: John Ashbery. Paris: Maeght, 1964.

Notes on Editors and Translators

Editors

ALEXANDER ASPEL. Professor of French literature and language at the State University of Iowa since 1946. He was born in 1908 in Estonia. A citizen of the United States since 1952, he holds degrees from the University of Tartu and the University of Paris. He has taught at the Ecole Nationale des langues orientales vivantes, the Cours de civilisation de la Sorbonne in Paris, and the University of Besançon as well as at Iowa.

An author of studies on Voltaire, Delacroix, and the French essayists, his special field of study in recent years has been the history of French literary style since Chateaubriand and contemporary French poetry; he has contributed to several literary publications in the United States, France, and Sweden. In 1962 he received the Chevalier de la Légion d'Honneur award from the French government.

DONALD JUSTICE. Has published two volumes of poetry, *The Summer Anniversaries,* which was the Lamont Poetry selection in 1959, and *A Local Storm* (1963) and was the editor of *The Collected Poems of Weldon Kees* as well as an assistant editor of *Midland,* an anthology of writing from the Writers Workshop of the University of Iowa, in which he teaches. He has contributed poems and criticism to many of the literary magazines of the United States—*Poetry, Harper's,* and *The New Yorker* among them—and his poetry is represented in numerous anthologies.

He was born in Miami, Florida, in 1925 and educated at the University of Miami, the University of North Carolina, Stanford University, and the University of Iowa, where he took his Ph.D.

Translators

PAULENE ASPEL. A native of France, Mrs. Aspel is associate professor of French at Iowa Wesleyan College, Mt. Pleasant. M.A. University of Paris, M.A. University of Iowa. She has published a volume of poetry, *Goût d'une Autre Terre* with Seghers, Paris, and poems and articles in such periodicals as *Botteghe Oscure, Parler, Western Review* and *French Review.*

CLARK BLAISE. Born in North Dakota in 1940, of French-Canadian extraction. He took his M.F.A. (master of fine arts) from the University of Iowa and teaches at the University of Wisconsin, Milwaukee. His short stories have appeared in *Silo, Shenandoah,* and *Chrysalis.*

WILLIAM BROWN. Born in Los Angeles, California, in 1939, he attended Calvin and Los Angeles State colleges and the Poetry Workshop at the University of Iowa.

WARREN CARRIER. Chairman of the English Department at Montana State University; he has taught at Portland State University, Bennington College, University of Iowa, and elsewhere. He has published poetry, fiction, and criticism. The author of two novels, *The Hunt* and *Bay of the Damned,* he has completed a new novel and a critical book on Joyce. He was co-editor, with Paul Engle, of *Reading Modern Poetry.*

JOSEPH DE ROCHE. Born in New Hampshire in 1938 and raised on the coast of Maine; he received a B.A. degree from Northeastern University in Boston. His poems have appeared in the *Beloit Poetry Journal* and *Poetry Northwest.*

HARRY DUNCAN. Born in Keokuk, Iowa, he is the director of the Cummington Press and of the typography laboratory at the University of Iowa. Translator from several languages; librettist; the author of "Poems and Translations," *Poets of Today I.*

Notes on Editors and Translators

PAUL ENGLE. Born in Cedar Rapids, Iowa, in 1908. B.A. Coe College, M.A. University of Iowa, B.A., M.A., Oxford University (Rhodes Scholar). Published nine volumes of poetry (*American Child, Word of Love, Poems in Praise, A Woman Unashamed*), a novel. Editor *O. Henry Prize Stories*. Published in *Poetry, New Yorker, Kenyon Review*, etc. Director, Program in Creative Writing, University of Iowa.

RALPH FREEDMAN. Born in Hamburg, Germany, in 1920, emigrated to England, 1939, to the United States, 1940. He received his Ph.D. from Yale in 1954 and has been teaching in the English Department at the University of Iowa since 1953. The author of many articles, essays, and reviews, he published a novel, *Divided,* in 1948, and a book of criticism, *The Lyrical Novel,* in 1963.

DONALD JUSTICE. Born in Miami, Florida, in 1925. He is the author of *The Summer Anniversaries,* the Lamont Poetry Selection, 1959, and *A Local Storm;* editor of *The Collected Poems of Weldon Kees;* and associate professor of English, University of Iowa.

DORI KATZ. A native of Belgium, she has been a member of the Poetry Workshop at the University of Iowa, where she received the M.F.A. degree.

EDMUND KEELEY. Born of American parents in Damascus, Syria, in 1928, he was educated at Princeton University and Wadham College, Oxford. He is associate professor, English Department, Princeton University. He was a visiting lecturer at the Program in Creative Writing, University of Iowa, in 1962–63 and has published two novels, two volumes of translation, and numerous stories, articles, and reviews in American, British, and Greek quarterlies.

DAVID LUNDE. Born in Berkeley, California, in 1941, he moved at age five to Dharan, Saudi Arabia, where his family still resides. He took his B.A. degree from Knox College.

MAURICE O'MEARA. Born in 1934, he received his M.A. and Ph.D. from the University of Iowa. He was a Fulbright scholar at Montpellier, France, in 1958–59, and teaches French at the University of Iowa.

TOD PERRY. Formerly of New York City, he took his M.F.A. at the University of Iowa. He has taught in Puerto Rico and has published poetry in *Epoch, New Yorker,* and elsewhere.

DAVID PRYCE-JONES. Born in Vienna in 1936, he spent much of his childhood in France and Austria. Educated at Eton and Magdalen College, Oxford, he published his first novel, *Owls and Satyrs,* in 1961, *The Sands of Summer* in 1963. He is a visiting lecturer at the Program in Creative Writing, University of Iowa.

ROSALIND SHERK. Born in New Zealand in 1939, she took her B.A. and M.A. at the University of Iowa. She has taught English at the University of South Carolina and Mary Rogers College in New York.

W. D. SNODGRASS. A native of Pennsylvania, he received his B.A. and M.F.A. from the University of Iowa and teaches at Wayne State University. He is the author of *Heart's Needle,* which was awarded the Pulitzer Prize for poetry, and has published both poetry and criticism in many magazines.

WILLIAM STAFFORD. Received his Ph.D. from the University of Iowa in 1953 and teaches at Lewis and Clark College in Oregon. He is the author of *West of Your City* and *Traveling Through the Dark,* which received the National Book Award in poetry in 1963.

JAMES STEPHENS. Born in Milwaukee, Wisconsin, in 1939. He is a member of the Poetry Workshop, University of Iowa.

RICHARD G. STERN. A native of New York City, he received his Ph.D. from the University of Iowa in 1954. He teaches at the University of Chicago and has published poems and translations from several languages as well as criticism. He is chiefly known for his novels, the most recent being *In Any Case*.

VINCENT STEWART. Born in San Augustine, Texas, in 1939. He has been working toward a Ph.D. at the University of Iowa. Teaches at Northeast Missouri State College, he was represented in *Iowa Workshop Poets / 1963*, and in many small poetry journals.

MARK STRAND. Born on Prince Edward Island, Canada, he was educated at Antioch College, Yale, and the University of Iowa, where he teaches in the Program in Creative Writing. He has published poems and translations in such magazines as *The Nation, Atlantic*, and *New Yorker*.

CHARLES P. WRIGHT, JR. Born in Pickwick Dam, Tennessee, in 1935, he took his M.F.A. at the University of Iowa. He has published poems and translations in *Carleton Miscellany, Massachusetts Review, Chelsea Review*, and elsewhere.

WAI-LIM YIP. A native of China and a poet in both Chinese and English, as well as a translator, he has published collections of his own poetry in Taiwan and has appeared in this country in *Trace* and the *Beloit Poetry Journal*.

Postface

By Paul Engle

Once upon a time, translation meant the direct removal of an earthly soul to heaven, without an intervening death.

Too often, in the translation of a poem from one language to another, the text suffers an actual death. The commonest cause of the fatality is linguistic competence without creative talent. Mere accuracy to the words in which a poem is written is not accuracy to the poem. Since the verse was not written as a linguistic or scholarly exercise, but as an imaginative response of a living man to his lived life, expressing his shock or delight, his suspicion or praise, some imagination must be mixed with a translation if it is to be true.

Believing that a little help can be given to young writing students, the University of Iowa has established "Workshops" in fiction and in poetry. The result has been to bring there a steady annual increment of young men and women whose essential concern was not only the study of literature, but an elementary effort at making it. A surprising number of these had a deep interest in another language, this being an age in which people move from one side of the earth to another as easily as they once moved to the next town.

In recognition of this new development in university life, a "Translation Workshop" was added to the others, so that those who knew languages could work with those who were trying to become writers, or were already established. The Translation Workshop was first taught by Edmund Keeley, now at Princeton University, and later by Mark Strand and Fred Will.

In that workshop, students familiar with Greek, Chinese, Bengali, Korean, German, Polish, Gaelic, Spanish, Italian, Japanese, or French received help from those who knew the forms, tortures, felicities, supple varieties, and curious exactitudes of the English language. This collection came from such a combining of the linguistic with the creative. The extraordinary flexibility and range of an American state university allowed so diverse a group of poets, linguists, critics, and scholars to join in such an enterprise.

The selection of poems to be translated was made solely by Professor Alexander Aspel, of the Department of Romance Languages, who brought together scholarly skill, critical judgment, and the most penetrating insights about poetry.

The translations were supervised by Professor Donald Justice, himself a poet of subtle mind, from the staff of The Program in Creative Writing. His problems were many, but this not being one man's book, he could share them with the Poetry and Translation Workshops and with so sympathetic a man as Professor Aspel. Professor Justice, however, finally had to give to each of these translations the sort of devoted care that he might well have been giving to his own poetry.

The first problem was the nature of the poets to be translated. They were of a great complexity, having in common numerous tough qualities: a drive to push beyond surrealism, an ironical suspicion of experience, a language loaded with ordinary details mingled with the most acute intuitions, a wish to make poetry itself an order of reality, and a determination to write the poem largely as a sequence of distinct images, often without transitions or comments.

This meant enormous care in realizing not only the plain sense of a word, but also its implications, for this is poetry in which meaning is less stated than hinted. René Char wrote, "I took my head as one takes a lump of salt, and literally pulverized it." From these pieces came the poem. Thus, the meaning was to be found less in a general summing up than in the unexpressed tension between the particles of the poem.

Another problem was the anthology's effort to present versions which were lively poems in English, rhythmical and attractive in sound, having a tone that did not reek of the translator's sweat. It was hoped that poets who had tried to bring these qualities into their own verse, might be able to achieve them in translations from the verse of others. Hoped!

Every translation is a failure.

By attempting to produce texts that had as close a sense of original poetry in English as possible, this anthology tried to reduce the degree of failure. The most scrupulous care for the French original and the most imaginative manipulation of the English language were demanded. Not all twenty-four translators had a perfect knowledge of French, so that a procedure had to be worked out which would prevent gross error and at the same time take advantage of their skill in handling their own native tongue.

In most instances, literal versions were prepared, often to the accompaniment of discussions, at all times nimble, at some times violent, of variant meanings. Then the poet would write out his English verse and send copies to Donald Justice and Alexander Aspel, who would then exchange views of the successes and failures. Often, several exchanges between editors and poets would be necessary. In the latter stages of the book, when Justice was in San Francisco and Aspel in Paris, the letters were frequent, lengthy, and agonizing, as tiny points had to be settled over such lengths of space and time. A line from Char, for example, was given six different versions before the inevitable compromise was reached.

Every translation was thus scrutinized at least twice, once for linguistic accuracy and once for the pleasure of its sound in English. The most difficult aspect of all was striking a balance between what the poet had seemed to intend in French, and what the translator in his own freedom could find as equivalents in English. How should the verb "se mêle" be carried over, when its subject was the approach of night at a street corner? Far more cunningly contrived images than those used by more conventional poets had to be given their own proper subtleties in English phrases not always designed for such purposes. The test always had to be accuracy to the intention of the poet, as far as it could be discovered, rather than an exact transliteration of his vocabulary.

To make a book by group effort is both difficult and dangerous, but it has the enormous advantage of bringing several differing sensibilities into play on a single poem, frequently with results one person alone would not reach. The individual translator, however, was given great liberty, so that the collection would not sound like the bland work of a committee.

Many of the French poets were themselves translators from various languages, and thus less suspicious of their own work being violated than might have been expected. Because of his fortunate presence in France, Professor Aspel was able to check various details personally with Francis Ponge, René Char, Pieyre de Mandiargues, and Jacques Dupin. How pleasant to have done this book in Paris, where every poem could have been verified by the poet!

As the world shrinks, the need for translation expands. It seems likely that, for the rest of the twentieth century, each country will have not one but two literatures: the one produced by its own writers, and the other translated from the world's languages. This secondary literature will often have the most immediate and energizing effect on writers of the language into which it has been translated. Therefore, the more it seems like a primal text in its own right, the greater effect it will have. To recognize this trend is the purpose of the Translation Workshop at the University of Iowa, and of this book.